THE
ONLINE
Millionaire

THE
ONLINE
Millionaire

Strategies for Building a Web-Based Empire on eBay and Beyond

AMY JOYNER

BICENTENNIAL
1807
WILEY
2007
BICENTENNIAL

John Wiley & Sons, Inc.

Published by John Wiley & Sons, Inc., Hoboken, New Jersey.
Published simultaneously in Canada.

For general information on our other products and services or for technical
support, please contact our Customer Care Department within the United States
at (800) 762-2974, outside the United States at (317) 572-3993 or fax (317) 572-4002.

Wiley also publishes its books in a variety of electronic formats. Some content that
appears in print may not be available in electronic books. For more information about
Wiley products, visit our web site at www.wiley.com.

Library of Congress Cataloging-in-Publication Data:

Joyner, Amy.
    The online millionaire : strategies for building a web-based empire on eBay and
    beyond / Amy Joyner ; developed by Literary Productions.
        p.   cm.
    Includes index.
    ISBN-13 978-0-471-78674-0 (cloth)
    ISBN-10 0-471-78674-8 (cloth)
        1. Electronic commerce.   2. Internet marketing.   3. Internet auctions.
    4. Success in business.   5. eBay (Firm)   I. Literary Productions.   II. Title.
    HF5548.32.J69   2007
    658.8'7—dc22

                                                                            2006030760

Printed in the United States of America.

10   9   8   7   6   5   4   3   2   1

To my darling son, Jackson.
Words can't convey how much I love you.

Contents

3 Auctions and Shopping on Yahoo!   **73**

4 Building Your Own Web Site   **101**

5 Other Auction Sites and Online Marketplaces   **123**

Introduction

The Internet is no longer an uncharted business frontier. In this day and age, every successful business understands the importance of having a strong Internet presence, whether you're a big manufacturing conglomerate or a small hometown retailer. The Internet can erase boundaries and extend your company's reach far beyond its local market. This is particularly true for retailers that can easily reach out to customers around the world to find a broader market for their products on the World Wide Web.

In 2006 alone, consumers spent $200 billion on Internet purchases. While some of that total includes travel booked online, the bulk of that amount, $138 billion, was spent on tangible goods, such as holiday gifts, products people use every day, and special treats that shoppers can't find locally. Online sales have doubled since 2003, and they continue to grow at an exciting pace every year. Without question, the Internet still provides one of the greatest opportunities for any entrepreneur.

As recently as just a few years ago, online entrepreneurs could make a successful go of it by hitching their fortunes to one of the existing online marketplaces, such as eBay or Yahoo!, but now, even the most successful sellers on those sites are looking to expand their businesses into other online channels to achieve maximum revenues and profits.

What's known as multichannel online marketing is the hottest thing going in cyberspace today, and it's no wonder. Even long-established businesses are experiencing dramatic and sustained spikes in sales as they expand into other online channels and fully harness the power of the Internet marketplace. Multichannel online marketing is how the world's wealthiest and savviest entrepreneurs operate, and those who have mastered this art have made huge fortunes.

This book will show you how to become the next huge online success story.

Your goal as an Internet entrepreneur should be to have a presence on every Web-based marketplace where your customers and potential customers shop. In *The Online Millionaire*, I'll introduce you to the most popular online channels and reveal the tricks of the trade for excelling in these marketplaces. You'll learn the ins and outs of selling on eBay, Amazon.com, Yahoo!, Overstock.com, and other auction marketplaces. You'll also read about how to use search engines and comparison-shopping sites to attract customers and drive sales. Plus, you'll find out how to go about building your own professional e-commerce store, along with proven ways to make money promoting other companies on your site.

At the end of every chapter, I profile sellers who have been particularly successful in that channel, but who also excel at multichannel marketing. These merchant-mentors share their own experiences and hands-on lessons for maximizing sales. As you read their stories, you'll notice a persistent theme: Though their businesses are all quite diverse, they are thriving thanks to their diversified approach to selling, and they're always looking for new opportunities to expand their reach through other marketplaces. These are businesspeople you should watch and mimic because each, in his or her own way, is on the leading edge of Internet marketing.

Each of the eight chapters focuses in depth on a particular online channel that you may want to consider for your business. The book opens with a chapter on eBay, which is by far the most popular and most frequently visited e-commerce marketplace in the world. EBay hosts millions of products from millions of sellers. It's the site that many turn to first when they need to buy something.

While it is still the 800-pound gorilla of e-commerce, as you'll realize by the time you reach the final pages of this book, online entrepreneurs now have many other options to reach buyers beyond eBay. With just a few clicks, you can also be up and running on sites like Amazon.com, Yahoo!, Overstock.com, and even your own proprietary store—if you know the right steps to follow. I'll show you exactly how to launch your own multichannel online marketing empire, regardless of the type of products you sell. You'll discover how each online channel works, what it costs to sell there, how to get started, and what products sell best.

What does it *really* take to build a thriving Internet empire? What's the optimum way to locate merchandise to sell? And how can you most effectively display items to attract the highest sales? The answers to these questions and more are yours to discover in *The Online Millionaire*, the first book ever to feature the proven and tested strategies for building a multichannel online marketing business that are actually being used by today's most successful e-commerce merchants.

The diverse businesses offer merchandise in a variety of product areas, including jewelry, gourmet foods, computer gear, electronics, home-improvement items, apparel, music, flowers, video games, movies, wedding favors, sports equipment, collectibles, housewares, and travel advice.

Every featured seller has enjoyed legendary and documented success, and most have built their online businesses from the ground up. They share such things as how they got started, how they locate and decide which merchandise to sell, how they've handled growth, how they ship goods most efficiently, how they keep customers happy, and much more. It's like gaining access to 15 different role models who will share their never-before-revealed business secrets learned from hard-earned experience.

That's what makes *The Online Millionaire* different from other how-to titles. It includes the stories and time-tested lessons of entrepreneurs who have demonstrated that they know what it takes to succeed in the online marketplace.

Among other things, you'll discover:

- How to build a significant Web-based business from the ground up.
- What it takes to generate enough revenue to create a full-time career selling items online through such sites as eBay, Amazon.com, Yahoo!, and Overstock.com.
- How to get your products and services listed on a variety of shopping sites—instead of just one.
- Which items sell best on which sites.
- How to cross-promote your merchandise among various selling platforms.
- Why product selection is so important, and how to choose the optimum mix of items for your site.
- The best tools to help automate your online business so you can concentrate on important things—like selling.
- Ways to increase your feedback rankings and product reviews, making buyers more inclined to do business with you.
- The biggest challenges even the most successful online merchants face and how to overcome them.
- Proven tips for most efficiently shipping goods to buyers around the world.
- How and when to expand your business into other types of merchandise.
- How to take advantage of all the perks the various sites offer their best sellers.
- The secrets to looking like a multimillion-dollar business, even if you're running everything from your living room or kitchen table.
- How to develop a process for making sure items sold are delivered on time and in good condition.

- Proven methods for creating a smoothly running system that allows product orders to be filled quickly and efficiently.

- The different options for pricing items—and which ones work best.

- Easy ways to build your own web site with little or no money.

- How to work with wholesalers and find great deals that can be sold at high margins.

Please don't close this book after you've read the final profile about Wendy Shepherd, an affiliate marketer pulling in loads of money simply by promoting other web sites. There are more tips yet to discover in the section titled "Fifty Keys to Becoming an Online Millionaire." This closing section highlights and summarizes the best business strategies espoused by those featured throughout the preceding chapters. The book also includes a handy list of resources that these highly successful merchants have used to propel their online empires, and I encourage you to visit my web site at www.TheOnlineMillionaire.com for more effective marketing strategies.

So, let's get started on this journey to creating a thriving online business that can put your company front and center on all of the world's top e-commerce sites.

How Multichannel Online Marketing Works

According to the most basic definition, multichannel marketing refers to having more than one channel of distribution for your products. It's certainly not a new concept. Offline companies often sell their products through multiple channels, including retail stores, mail order, and wholesale accounts.

In the Internet age, multichannel marketing takes on a whole new meaning. The Internet itself is a new channel of distribution for many bricks-and-mortar retailers. And on the Internet, there are literally hundreds, if not thousands, of channels where merchants can promote their products. Each channel is like a shopping mall with its own unique merchants' rules and fees. Every one appeals to a different sort of customer and draws a different buyer demographic.

This book focuses on eight channels, some of which are specific online marketplaces and others that are best characterized as marketing strategies. The marketplaces profiled within these pages—sites like eBay, Amazon.com, Yahoo!, Overstock.com, uBid, iOffer, and Half.com—represent only a fraction of those operating on the Internet. But they are among the most popular and viable marketplaces. These are the sites that the online millionaires recommend because of their ability to attract customers and drive sales.

Multichannel online retailers need to embrace not only alternative marketplaces, but also a variety of marketing strategies to attract customers. It's not enough these days to simply post auctions on eBay or put items up on a web site and wait for customers to come to you. Paid search-engine advertising campaigns should be a part of any online company's marketing budget, as pay-per-click ads are one of the best ways to capture customers and sales.

Comparison-shopping engines, which attract about 50 million interested buyers a month, are another marketing channel that shouldn't be overlooked. Consumers visit these sites to research purchases and find bargains. If your company and products aren't represented there, particularly around the holidays and other peak shopping seasons, you're missing out on untold potential sales. The comparison-shopping engines highlighted in *The Online Millionaire* stand above the competition in terms of accuracy and usefulness. Independent companies that track web site traffic rank Shopzilla, BizRate.com, Shopping.com, NexTag, Froogle, and PriceGrabber as the Web's most frequently visited and used comparison-shopping engines, hence their inclusion in this book.

Affiliate marketing is a final channel you may want to consider as you build your online business. In this book, you'll read about individuals who earn considerable income as affiliates, simply by referring business to other online companies. And you'll also read about affiliate marketing from the flip side, specifically how companies increase their revenues by hiring affiliates to advertise and promote their products. Affiliate marketing is quite an interesting and lucrative field from both the merchant and affiliate perspective. Most big online retailers, including Amazon and eBay, use affiliates to capture incremental sales. Many huge web sites function as affiliates for popular brands, earning commissions every time they refer a sale to those online retailers. Depending on the type of business you're in, you may be able to earn income as an affiliate for other companies and create a network of affiliates who drive business to your site.

As an online merchant, you should strive to have a presence everywhere your potential customers shop. That's really the goal of multichannel online marketing. Be everywhere your customers are, and your business will thrive.

Using This Book

This book is divided into eight chapters, each representing a different online marketing channel. Chapter 1 offers an overview of how to master sales on eBay, still the most influential and popular e-commerce site. Chapter 2 reveals how to get your products listed and sold through Amazon.com, which is proving to be a growing source of revenue for many online merchants. Chapter 3 discusses the many advantages of setting up a shopping and auction business through Yahoo!, while Chapter 4 reveals the steps you'll need to take in building your own e-commerce web site. Chapter 5 profiles numerous online auctioneers and similar listing sites that compete with eBay to offer sellers alternative outlets for reaching buyers. Chapter 6 discusses successful paid and natural search-engine marketing techniques, while Chapter 7 shows how to get your products listed in the various comparison-shopping search engines. Finally, Chapter 8 offers the lowdown on advertising and affiliate programs, which allow merchants to earn added revenue for referring business to other web sites.

For the most part, the eight chapters follow the same easy-to-read and understand structure. Each chapter opens with a lowdown on the particular channel. That's where you'll learn the history of the site and find statistical information about its demographic reach and sales potential.

This is followed by specific instructions and tips for getting started selling in the channel. You'll then learn more about how the sales process works in the channel, from marketing to buying to shipping. The next section in most chapters is a definite must-read. It discusses items and product lines that sell best in that channel, as well as those that don't usually work well. Finally, you'll read a frank commentary of the pros and cons of conducting business in the channel to help you determine whether it's an appropriate market-place for your business. Each chapter then offers an action plan that you can follow if you want to start selling in that channel.

And at the conclusion of every chapter, you'll read the stories of one, two, or three online entrepreneurs who are successfully marketing their products through the featured channel. These merchants reveal how they got started selling online, and they share their failures as well as their successes.

Now, grab your cursors and click your finger to the next page to learn step one to becoming a verifiable online millionaire.

1

Mastering eBay

Without a doubt, more entrepreneurial success stories begin on eBay than on any other online commerce site. EBay is the granddaddy of Internet marketplaces, both in age and in terms of the volume of goods sold every year.

The trading community founded by young Silicon Valley computer programmer Pierre Omidyar in 1995 has become the most popular shopping destination on the Internet. EBay now has more than 200 million registered users who buy and sell just about everything imaginable on the site—including homes, video games, antiques, collectibles, cars, clothing, boats, cameras, jewelry, crafts, and a host of professional services. In fact, shoppers will find about 55 million items in more than 50,000 categories for sale or auction at eBay at any given time. All told, users annually list about two billion items for sale on eBay, worth more than $44.3 billion. Both figures, by the way, have been growing annually, proving that even as eBay matures and more competitors enter the marketplace, the site remains a great place to go into business for yourself. EBay is by far the biggest, boldest, and most opportunity-laden e-commerce store the world has ever known.

While millions visit eBay every day to sell single items (or to buy them), for an increasing number of Americans, logging onto the site means going to work. A survey conducted by ACNielsen International Research on behalf of eBay revealed that more than 724,000 Americans report that eBay is their primary or secondary source of income. As more entrepreneurs have discovered the site's moneymaking potential and more businesses have begun selling on eBay as part of a multi-channel online marketing strategy, that number has increased 68 percent from just a few years ago. In addition to these professional eBay sellers, another 1.5 million people supplement their income by auctioning goods on the online site.

Getting Started

What's especially attractive to entrepreneurs of all sizes is how little time and money it takes to get started on eBay. (But remember this caveat: If you want to grow into one of eBay's most successful merchants, you'll eventually have to put in lots of long hours. All success requires hard work.) Because all sales are closed online, budding eBay entrepreneurs have the opportunity to set their own schedules, squeezing in time at the computer after work, after school, and after the kids are in bed. As a result, all sorts of folks—teenagers, stay-at-home moms, new college graduates, middle-aged workers, busy middle managers, and senior citizens, just to name a few—are in business on eBay, hawking almost every item imaginable.

Getting started as an eBay seller is incredibly simple. Many of eBay's most successful merchants—those who have been christened Titanium PowerSellers because their sales volume on the site totals at least $1.8 million annually—started out hawking items they had lying around the house. That was enough to kick-start their entrepreneurial dreams and set them on the road to success. That is how you should start, as well.

Unless you're already an established bricks-and-mortar or online merchant, don't begin hunting for inventory until you've first tested the eBay marketplace. And if you've never purchased anything through eBay, complete a few transactions as a customer before you start selling things. This serves two important purposes. First, you'll get a sense of how the site works, and specifically the bidding process. Unlike in traditional auctions, where the bidding begins as soon as the auctioneer gives the word, many eBay auctions don't attract bids until the final few minutes or even seconds. In fact, with eBay's proxy bidding system, it's not unusual for prices to skyrocket in those final, frantic minutes.

Testing out eBay as a buyer will also provide you the opportunity to build up your feedback score, which is what other buyers and sellers will use to determine if yours is a reputable, honest, and ethical business. Every eBay user starts out with a feedback score of zero. It's only through satisfactory transactions that your score begins to grow.

EBay designed its feedback ratings to give buyers and sellers a measure of comfort about doing business with someone they've never met before. After an auction closes, both the seller and the buyer have an opportunity to rate the person on the other end of the transaction and to post a short comment about them. Every positive comment from a unique user garners another feedback point. Negative comments subtract a point from a user's feedback score. With neutral comments, no points are lost or gained.

Most people are hesitant to buy from eBay sellers with negative or low feedback scores. On eBay, your feedback score is like your approval rating. It's important to have a history of positive transactions before you start offering goods for sale. If you don't have a good feedback score, chances are few people will bid on your auctions and your goods will sell for less than they're worth. But if you've built a good reputation as an eBay buyer, bidders are more likely to trust you, and your merchandise will sell for a higher price.

By beginning your eBay experience on the buying side, you'll also gain insights into how other merchants on the site do business. As you've already read, thousands of individuals and companies sell things on eBay and each handles transactions differently. When you're buying, you'll want to pay attention to how these sellers describe the items they're selling, what kind of photographs they use, what disclosures they include in their auction ads, what shipping services they offer, how much they charge for shipping, how well they respond to questions and complaints, what forms of payments they accept, how quickly they fulfill orders, how they package their shipments, and in what condition purchased items arrive. Just through simple observation, you'll get some ideas for best practices for your own eBay venture. (You'll probably also learn a few don'ts along the way, as well.)

Only once you've done an ample amount of buying on eBay and feel comfortable transacting in the marketplace should you begin selling.

EBay has an excellent audio tour on its web site that walks you through the selling process in step-by-step detail. I recommend that you check it out, as it really helps to simplify the process. To learn more, point your Web browser to http://pages.ebay.com/education/selling.html.

There is a market for just about everything on eBay. Somebody recently paid $510 for another person's 15 minutes of fame, for goodness' sake. But some items sell better than others, and some things command higher prices because the demand for them is higher. In the next section, you'll learn more about the top-selling items on eBay and how to identify moneymakers in your sales category. But it's always a good idea to do some preliminary market and marketplace research before stocking up on merchandise. (As you scout for items to sell, you may discover a great niche. That's what happened for Steve Grossberg, the owner of 1Busyman Discount Games, whose success story you'll read about later in this chapter.)

So, clean out your closets, buy yard sale treasures, scour the clearance racks at your local department store, ask friends for their throwaways, or strike a deal with a local company to purchase its excess inventory on the cheap. Then, put one or two inexpensive items up for bid. That way, you can get a taste of the whole eBay selling process—

from posting to shipping—without getting overwhelmed with the workload or spending a lot of money.

Figuring out what to sell on eBay is the hardest part. After that, things get much easier. Unlike with most other entrepreneurial endeavors, eBay start-up costs are low. At the bare minimum, you'll need a computer with an Internet connection. Spring for high-speed Internet access, which will improve your efficiency and make uploading photographs of your items much easier.

A computer is all you really need in order to sell on eBay. But serious eBay sellers recommend that you invest in a few additional office supplies, including a digital camera, auction management software, and shelving or another organizational system for inventory management.

These days, it's crucial to include a photograph—and sometimes multiple pictures—of any item you list for auction. Online buyers can't touch the item or test out its features, so they rely on photography to have confidence they're bidding on a quality product.

If you have a regular camera, when you drop the film off for developing you can ask the lab to make and save digital copies of your pictures on a compact disk (CD). You can then incorporate those digital images into your eBay auction with relative ease.

But if you plan to do a lot of selling online, your best bet is to invest in a digital camera that allows you to quickly and easily transfer images to your computer hard drive.

When buying a digital camera, look for one that has image capture capabilities of *at least* two megapixels. Also choose a camera with macro capabilities, which will enable you to take close-up pictures without losing focus or distorting the image. Prices for digital cameras are dropping, and you'll find great deals for them online at eBay and other sites. For $200 to $300, you're likely to find a camera that will function well for your business.

In addition to the digital camera, you may want to invest in special lighting and white or neutral-colored backgrounds to give your auction photographs a professional look. A flatbed scanner is a good tool to have if you're selling items like books, CDs, photographs, baseball cards, or other flat items. A scanner produces sharper images of flat items than a digital camera will.

Finally, you'll need to sign up for a PayPal account, so you can send and receive money securely and quickly online. If you're intent on selling a lot on eBay, go for a Premier or Business account, which will enable you to receive credit and debit card payments online for a small fee. You will choose a user ID and password, and will be required to enter some personal data, including your address and telephone number. Once you've completed your PayPal registration, it's a good idea to have your account verified by adding a confirmed bank account. (You'll do this by providing a valid bank account number.) Once your account is verified, PayPal will lift your sending and withdrawal limits and allow you to send payments instantly using a checking account. As a Premier or Business account holder, you're also eligible for a PayPal ATM and debit card.

How It Works

EBay is a platform where merchants, both small and large, can sell goods and (sometimes) services to other individuals and businesses. Its reach is worldwide. EBay is open to buyers and sellers in dozens of countries—virtually anyplace with Internet access. The site was conceived as an open marketplace, where supply and consumer demand would determine prices. Auctions still proliferate on the site, but there are many more ways to buy and sell on eBay now than there were 12 years ago. EBay also gives its merchants the opportunity to sell items at fixed prices, open their own online stores, and market to customers who are looking to buy new items in a more conventional e-commerce environment.

EBay itself sells nothing tangible—just traffic and space on one of the Internet's most popular web sites. The company makes money through listing fees—what it charges merchants to advertise their items for sale—and by taking a commission on every item that successfully changes hands on eBay. The actual commission amount depends on the type of item that is sold and on the final bid price for that item, but it ranges from 5.25 percent of the final bid price on up.

What makes strangers comfortable completing transactions online? Feedback, which is eBay's version of the Better Business Bureau. As noted, after every completed transaction, buyers and sellers have the option of rating one another and commenting about their shared experience. EBay users can give one another a positive rating (which earns them one point), a negative rating (which costs them one point), or a neutral rating (no points). All those points are added up into a cumulative feedback score, which is one measure potential customers can use to determine if they want to buy from a seller. Another important component of the feedback score is the percentage of positive transactions that a user has been involved in. In order to be eligible for certain perks on eBay, sellers must maintain a certain feedback percentage. For example, PowerSellers must have at least a 98 percent positive feedback rating, as must those users wanting to sell through the new eBay Express.

As mentioned earlier, there are several ways to sell on eBay. Most people begin by selling items through competitive auctions where interested buyers bid against one another and drive up the price until time runs out. Auctions run for a set amount of time—either one, three, five, seven, or ten days. You set the starting bid for your auctions. This is one of the most important decisions you'll make because it will likely affect your profitability and the interest level in your auctions. Even now as eBay has become more competitive, many sellers prefer to start the bidding for their auctions at 99 cents and allow the market to establish the final price. This seems a scary proposition to many merchants who fear they'll be forced to sell a product for less than they paid for it. This can certainly happen, but in many product categories, demand is strong enough to support such a pricing strategy. One way to determine if this strategy can work for you is to check your competitors' listings to see how they price their items. You can also use

Market Research tools on eBay (or from third-party companies) to see how much identical items have closed for in the past. This information will help you make smart decisions about how to price your own merchandise, and you'll also be able to evaluate whether you're paying a fair wholesale price for it.

EBay allows you as a seller to set a reserve, the minimum price you're willing to accept. If no bid matches or tops the reserve, you don't have to sell the item. But remember that eBay assesses an extra fee for reserve-price auctions, and you can't recoup this fee if your item doesn't sell. Many successful eBay sellers believe that reserves are a bad idea because they can make the bidding process frustrating for potential buyers. When someone places a bid for an item, he or she likes to know that he or she has a chance of winning the auction at that price. But if you have a reserve, a potential buyer could place dozens of bids and still not reach that hidden minimum. And in all likelihood, the buyer will tire of the game and search for another seller who is offering the same product without a reserve. Rather than using reserves, most veteran sellers prefer to start bidding at (or very near) their must-get minimum. While these auctions may not garner as many bids as those starting at 99 cents, they have a higher likelihood of closing than reserve-price auctions. Remember, they cost less, too, because there are no reserve fees.

In addition to auctioning off merchandise, some eBay retailers choose to sell goods at a fixed price, also known as a "Buy It Now" price that they set. This allows the customer to immediately purchase the item with a single mouse click, instead of waiting for an auction to run its course. Many sellers like using the Buy It Now feature because they're able to turn more merchandise more quickly and are better able to regulate their profits. In 2006, eBay launched a new feature, called eBay Express, that is more like a traditional online store. EBay Express was designed to appeal to shoppers looking to buy new items—without the wait—in a marketplace similar to Amazon.com. An eBay Express shopper can fill a shopping cart with items from as many as five different eBay merchants and make a single payment to purchase them. EBay divvies up the payment among the five sellers, who then independently ship the items to the buyer.

To be eligible to sell on eBay Express, users must have a feedback score of at least 100 and a 98 percent positive rating. In addition, they need a PayPal Premier or PayPal Business account to receive payments. When sellers meet these requirements, new items listed in most categories will automatically be posted on eBay Express, as well as on eBay. (EBay Express also includes some listings for used items, specifically antiques, art, some business and industrial items, certain collectibles, and vintage toys.) If you want your items to show up in the eBay Express inventory, be sure to post them in the fixed price format, instead of the auction format, or list them for sale in your eBay store. In addition, you must include a photograph and provide information about the item condition and shipping costs.

In addition to these methods, merchants also have the option of setting up an eBay store that they stock with fixed-price inventory. Many volume sellers do this to reduce their eBay fees. Instead of forking over a hefty insertion fee for each item, sellers pay just a few pennies to put a product on the shelves of their virtual store. EBay charges as little as 5 cents per item for a 30-day store listing. Sellers also pay a monthly subscription fee, ranging from $15.95 a month to $499.95 a month, to operate a store. When an item sells, they pay a final value fee, ranging from 10 percent of the item's selling price on up.)

All items in an eBay store are sold at a fixed price, with no bidding, and listings have a longer duration. A store is a good place to sell lower-priced or low-margin goods because you avoid the high insertion fees that can eat into profits. But such items may be harder for potential buyers to find because they don't always show up in normal search results. For this reason, many eBay merchants choose to list some items for auction and place others for sale in their store to guarantee the broadest possible reach.

Take the example of A City Discount. This Titanium PowerSeller sells new and used restaurant equipment. High-ticket items are sold through auctions, but accessory items, like food processor blades, can openers, and food scales are sold in the company's eBay store. Potential buyers can access A City Discount's store through any of its eBay auctions and by searching specifically for eBay store items.

Now that you know about the different ways to sell merchandise on eBay, it's time for a primer on how to advertise those items to your customers. At the very least, every auction, fixed-price, or store listing should include a photograph and detailed description of the item for sale. It's also a good idea to include:

- *Payment terms.* Will you accept personal checks and money orders? Do you accept money through PayPal, the eBay-owned online payment site, and other similar services? How long does a winning bidder have to pay for the auction?
- *Shipping and handling charges.* EBay offers a shipping calculator that you can easily integrate into your auctions.
- *Shipping terms.* Buyers like to know how quickly an item will be shipped once they've paid for it.
- *Your return policy.*
- *Your contact information.* Bidders need to know how to contact you if they have a question about an item or a sale.
- *Answers to frequently asked questions (FAQs).* As your eBay business grows, you'll notice that bidders often ask the same questions. Preempt these queries by including a FAQ section in each auction listing.

There are many things that you can do to add oomph to your auction listings and improve your visibility in the crowded marketplace. The customized listing options are myriad, but a few are most commonly used and provide the greatest impact for the least amount of money.

Some sellers pay an extra 50 cents to add a subtitle to their auctions or an extra $1 so their auction headline shows up in bold text. Adding a gallery image is another popular choice, and it costs just 35 cents. A gallery image is a small picture that appears in the eBay category listings and search pages. It allows customers to see a photograph of what you have for sale without clicking on your auction. These days, it's really a must. When searching for an item, potential buyers are likely to be faced with dozens, if not hundreds, of options. A high-quality gallery image, paired with a descriptive title, increases the likelihood that these shoppers will click through to view your item and perhaps bid on it rather than an item offered by the competition.

If you really want to stand out, you can buy featured placement for your auctions (at a cost of $5 to $39.95) or by using eBay's keywords program to purchase ads that appear at the top of search results pages. For a list of the various options and specific fees, visit eBay's seller help pages at http://pages.ebay.com/help/sell/fees.html.

Once you close a sale on eBay, you're responsible for collecting payment and shipping the merchandise to the buyer in a timely manner. Many eBay sellers accept checks, money orders, and credit cards. But the most popular payment method on eBay is PayPal, which allows for the immediate electronic transfer of funds from buyer to seller. You will discover that if you don't offer PayPal as a payment option, you'll lose out on business and experience delays in being able to ship items. As online retailing has become more efficient, the delivery expectations of customers have risen. In general, they expect items purchased online to be shipped within a few days and to arrive within a few more days. Try to create a fulfillment system to meet these expectations. Process and ship your online orders the day they're received (or the day after) and offer quick-delivery services, like Priority Mail, FedEx Ground, or United Parcel Service (UPS)'s two- or three-day options. If you cannot meet these standards, clearly spell out your shipping terms in every eBay listing so your customers aren't surprised or enraged by the delays.

One of the best things you can do to make your life as an online merchant easier is to invest in automation software that helps you manage your inventory and listings in the various online marketplaces. EBay offers several options, including the free Turbo Lister and the subscription-based Selling Manager, Blackthorne Basic, and Blackthorne Pro. There are also many third-party companies that sell auction-management packages. You'll find a listing of them in the Resources section of this book under "Channel Management and Automation Software." The top auction management systems give you the capability to create listing templates, bulk list items for sale, manage inventory, process payments, answer customer e-mails, print packing slips and package labels, and integrate with your shipping company. Unfortunately, there's no single "best" solution, as you'll learn from reading the seller profiles that accompany this chapter. You'll need to evaluate the various software solutions to find the most affordable one that suits your business. As you shop around for tools to automate your eBay business, be sure to find out what other marketplaces the software supports. As you expand your online venture into additional channels, it's important to have computer systems and infrastructure that work seamlessly for each marketplace.

What Sells Best

What sells best on eBay? That is the multimillion-dollar question. Fortunately, there's no single answer. Entrepreneurs have achieved phenomenal success selling a variety of merchandise on eBay, from the super cheap to the super expensive. You'll find Platinum and Titanium PowerSellers hawking everything, including 99-cent charm bracelets, video games, B movies, athletic shoes, designer apparel, CDs, musical instruments, cameras, high-end computers, rare antiques, houses, pet supplies, expensive jewelry, luxury cars, and everything in between. Someone even tried to sell an entire town on eBay!

You can try to sell anything on the site, but success depends on the competitiveness of the particular marketplace for your products, how your items are priced for sale, and your required profit margin, which takes into account your acquisition and selling expenses.

You need look no further than eBay's financial results to find out what items are the top sellers and moneymakers on the site. In 1998, eBay's first year as a public company, the site hosted 13.6 million auctions and the value of all goods traded reached just $306 million. Now, eBay has 10 separate merchandise categories that generate $1 billion or more in annual auction sales each. The biggest is eBay Motors ($7.5 billion), which includes sales of vehicles, car parts, and accessories. Other top-grossing categories are consumer electronics ($2.6 billion); computers ($2.4 billion); books, movies, and music ($2 billion); clothing and accessories ($1.8 billion); sports ($1.8 billion); collectibles ($1.5 billion), toys ($1.5 billion); home and garden ($1.3 billion); and jewelry and gemstones ($1.3 billion).

For a more detailed examination of eBay best sellers, turn to the monthly Hot Categories Report (available online at http://pages.ebay .com/sellercentral/hotitems.pdf) to see the fastest-growing sales categories on the site. The eBay Pulse at http://pulse.ebay.com provides a daily snapshot of "current trends, hot picks, and cool stuff on eBay." The eBay Pulse lists the most-searched-for items. What's hot right now? Designer handbags, new Xbox and Sony PlayStation video game systems, and iPods. The Pulse also ranks the site's largest stores, based on the volume of listings.

Pros and Cons

EBay emerged on the e-commerce scene as a boundless flea market. In the beginning, that reputation was well deserved, as eBay was overrun with people buying and selling collectibles and used goods. But in the 12 years since its founding, eBay has evolved into a worldwide marketplace for all sorts of goods—new and used, unique and everyday, cheap and expensive. It's this diversity that gives eBay its biggest advantage in the online marketplace and yet provides the biggest drawback for its merchants.

No store in the world—not even Wal-Mart—offers the wealth and variety of merchandise that eBay does. You can find virtually anything there. Things that were previously considered rare or hard to find are often available in abundance on eBay from sellers around the world. For that reason, eBay is the preeminent online shopping site, the one that consumers think of first when there's something they need to buy. No other online auctioneer or e-commerce site can deliver the customers that eBay does. Literally millions of users log in every day to see what's for sale and to place bids on items. That's a virtually limitless audience of buyers.

You might ask, What more could an online entrepreneur want? The answer, quite simply, is less competition.

EBay's huge audience of buyers also attracts a huge base of sellers. No other online site is populated with more competing merchants than eBay. As a seller on eBay, you have the potential to reach an unbelievable number of bidders, but you're also facing fierce competition from others selling the *exact same* merchandise, sometimes for the same price, or even much less. Therefore, items on eBay are more likely to become commodities, making it even tougher to command high prices for them.

Competition is particularly cutthroat in such categories as movies, music, and electronics. The merchants who succeed in these categories do so because they have stellar customer service, extremely low operating costs, efficient operations, and high profit margins.

Another disadvantage of eBay is its fee structure. You'll pay a small fee for at least every item you list for sale there, whether someone actually buys it or not. Plus, you must share a portion of the proceeds from each sale with eBay. In recent years, eBay has hiked its fees several times, making it more expensive and less profitable to sell on the site. These fee hikes raised the ire of eBay sellers both big and small, including some of the most successful Titanium PowerSellers, forcing many to shift more of their sales to alternate channels.

Some sellers also chafe at the fact that they essentially have to pay eBay twice for the same transaction when buyers pay using PayPal. (PayPal, which is owned by eBay, charges professional-level sellers a percentage fee for every auction payment it processes.)

The bottom line is this: Anyone who wants to become a successful online merchant definitely should have a presence on eBay, and perhaps a fairly significant presence. But, as more and more sellers are discovering every day, it's unwise to sell exclusively in one online marketplace. After achieving some success on eBay, many merchants opt to build their own e-commerce web sites to cultivate repeat business from existing customers. By doing so, they avoid having to share a percentage of revenue from every sale with eBay. Instead, that money becomes income instead of an expense.

Other channels, such as Amazon and Overstock, will provide you access to a different customer base, including many people who never have and never will buy through eBay. In an effort to compete with the Goliath that is eBay, these other channels often charge lower fees. Sellers find that attractive because it improves their profit margins.

To learn more about eBay's inner workings and detailed strategies for succeeding on the site from some of its most successful Titanium PowerSellers, I encourage you to get a copy of my book, *The eBay Millionaire* (John Wiley & Sons, 2005). It's available at bookstores everywhere or by visiting my web site at www.TheOnlineMillionaire.com.

Action Plan

Here are the steps for getting your eBay business up and running:

- ✔ If you haven't already done so, register as a user on eBay and check out the site's various tutorials and extensive help pages to find out how to navigate this vast marketplace.
- ✔ Begin familiarizing yourself with the buying and selling process by searching and bidding on items. Pay attention to how various sellers promote their items with photography, titles, headlines, and search-result features. Notice the categories where various items are listed.
- ✔ Win a few auctions (or Buy It Now sales), so you can see firsthand how other merchants handle postsale communications with buyers and how they package and ship merchandise.

✔ Diligently leave feedback for those sellers with whom you do business, and ask that they do the same for you. Strive for friendly, positive transactions so your feedback rating climbs.

✔ Decide what you're going to sell, using your own marketing smarts combined with the various market research tools available from eBay and other companies.

✔ Invest in any necessary equipment—a computer with a high-speed Internet connection, a scanner (if necessary), a digital camera, and photo backdrops and lighting.

✔ Download eBay's free bulk-listing tool, Turbo Lister, or invest in other software that will help you manage and automate your online auctions and sales.

✔ Within your software, create templates that you'll use every time you list an item for sale. Include basic information about your company, shipping costs, and policies and any other pertinent information that buyers may need.

✔ Experiment with various pricing strategies in your merchandise category to determine which one works best for your business. You'll want to find a pricing strategy that delivers the most customers while also maintaining a healthy bottom line for your business. You may find that you have to use different pricing methods for different types of merchandise.

✔ Don't just rely on auctions. Use eBay's Buy It Now feature to sell some items—perhaps those with a fairly stable market price but that are in high demand. Open up an eBay store to sell complementary or low-cost items without incurring high listing fees.

eBay Success Story

1Busyman Discount Games

In the late 1990s, Steve Grossberg wanted nothing more than to assemble a high-end set of golf clubs. So, he began buying drivers, woods, and putters from eBay and other online sites, seeking the best sticks at the best prices. After playing a few rounds with each of the clubs, he put the ones he liked most in his bag and resold the rest where he bought them—on eBay.

Grossberg's golf score dropped, and he started making money online, often reselling the rejected golf clubs for more than he paid for them in the first place.

A career salesman for R.J. Reynolds Tobacco Company, Grossberg was amazed by his online profits. A few years later, when he learned that Microsoft and Nintendo were launching two new video game systems in time for Christmas, Grossberg positioned himself to leverage the high demand and eBay's profit-making potential in this area as well.

"Knowing that you can buy things and sell them on eBay for more than you paid, I had the foresight to reserve a bunch of these different video game units in retail stores," he says. Grossberg paid full price for the video game systems, and when stock ran low at stores he began putting them up for auction on eBay. The 30 units he bought each sold for well above the purchase price, spurring Grossberg to begin considering eBay as more than just a casual sideline.

With his wife pregnant with their third child, Grossberg decided that eBay could provide just enough extra income to allow her to quit her job as a registered nurse and stay at home with the new baby. Given his success selling Microsoft Xbox and Nintendo GameCube systems, Grossberg set up meetings with video game distributors in New York and convinced them to take him on as an account. Because his initial investment was low—just $1,000 to $2,000—some of the large distributors refused to sell to Grossberg because he wasn't ordering enough to make the relationship profitable. Those distributors that did agree to sell to Grossberg charged him higher prices than their bigger-volume accounts. But Grossberg accepted these terms in order to break into what he knew to be a lucrative market. (More than $11 billion is spent annually on video games.)

After he'd proven himself as a legitimate online retailer, Grossberg was able to negotiate better wholesale prices with his suppliers.

Once he'd been in operation for a year or two, several distributors even solicited his business because they saw him as a lucrative and worthwhile customer.

Grossberg never intended for his eBay business to generate more than just a little extra spending money. He didn't even anticipate replacing his wife's nursing salary. His goal simply was to "make a few extra hundred dollars a month."

In the first year, 1Busyman Discount Games did just that, selling 700 games on eBay. But the next year, in 2003, that total skyrocketed to 33,500 items, and the sideline became a burgeoning business. Today, it's a full-time operation for Grossberg, and 1Busyman Discount Games ranks as the number-one discount video game store on eBay.

Great timing, smart buying decisions, niche marketing, automation, clever pricing strategies, and now a multichannel selling approach, have all played a role in Grossberg's success.

Admittedly, Grossberg set up shop on eBay at the perfect time—around 2002—when competition in the video game category was less intense than it is now. The cost of entry was low, too. Grossberg had to spend only a few thousand dollars to get started. "It would require a much bigger investment to launch the company the way I did now," Grossberg says. "To be a serious player on eBay today, you'd need $50,000 to $100,000 for inventory." That said, Grossberg believes opportunities still exist in other merchandise categories without spending so much up front.

From the very beginning of his online venture, Grossberg has been smart about the types of video games he sells. He does not try to compete against stores like Wal-Mart, Best Buy, or E.B. Games by selling new releases. Instead, he stocks only games that are no longer available in most stores. Although he sells games of all stripes, for players of all ages and skill levels, Grossberg distinguishes himself from competitors by offering hard-to-find games for children, featuring such characters as SpongeBob Square Pants, Dora the Explorer, and members of the *Sesame Street* gang. In all, he stocks about 450 stock-keeping units (SKUs), or products in inventory—all games that are at least six months past their release dates. The games are new, in original packaging, and available for all major gaming systems, including PlayStation, Xbox, GameCube, and GameBoy. Most importantly, they are sold at huge discounts.

Grossberg likes to keep about two to three months' supply on hand. In fact, he won't purchase a video game title unless he can buy dozens of copies at once. "I'm very deep in a lot of these games," he says. "You've got to have the courage to buy 200 or 300 of the same item. The worst thing is not being able to get any more of a good-selling game. If we don't have a game in stock, we can't sell it again."

Maintaining a deep inventory—as opposed to a broad one—makes his business more efficient, as well. He's doesn't have to constantly create listings for new products.

Selling older games gives Grossberg two distinct advantages. First, he avoids having to worry about competing with the likes of Wal-Mart and other big-box retailers that get volume discounts and can afford to put new-release video games on sale or offer them as loss leaders to get customers in their stores. Profit margins are also higher for older games because distributors often discount them to clear the way for newer titles. As a result, Grossberg's own net profit margin for his online sales averages a healthy 12 percent.

Though he sells thousands of video games every month, Grossberg isn't a gamer himself. This has allowed him to stay objective about the products he sells. He bases his buying decisions on how many units of a game will sell, not on whether it's fun to play. It is a bad idea to become too emotionally invested in what you're selling, Grossberg says, because doing so can inhibit your ability to turn a profit. For example, when Grossberg was a fledgling seller on eBay, he struck up a friendship with another video game merchant.

"He was a younger kid and a big video game addict," Grossberg recalls. "This guy would only buy games that he thought were good to play. His sales suffered as a result. His knowledge of video games probably hurt him. By contrast, I determine if it's a good game to stock because of how well it sells."

Most new-release video games sell for upwards of $50, but 1Busyman Discount's average selling price is a much lower $15. "It gives us a great niche market to sell games you can't get elsewhere. And, remember, it's a worldwide market," notes Grossberg, who counts on international sales for about 20 percent of his revenues. "When you get to a lower price point, there is a tremendous amount of demand."

Unlike many online sellers, who are slow to automate their listing and shipping practices, Grossberg embraced this time-saving technology early on. He began using basic auction management software in 2002 and by 2004 had switched to the popular ChannelAdvisor software to manage his more than 800 weekly auctions and to set up his own online store.

Additionally, Grossberg hired a software developer to write a computer program that allows him to automate fulfillment and shipping. Previously, he spent hours every day making a handwritten list of what games to send to each buyer. Now, that process is automated into a spreadsheet, allowing Grossberg to quickly and easily print hundreds of shipping labels, each coded with the necessary item SKU. "Years ago, if I shipped 100 items a night, it would take me a lot of time," he says. "Now, I can ship 700 items a night. It's not that I'm working less than before I got automated. I'm working the same amount of time, but I'm selling more."

In Grossberg's category—video games—most items are sold at a fixed price in an eBay seller's store or through a Buy It Now transaction. Traditional auctions aren't effective for commodity items like video games. Sellers who try that approach often find that they lose money on each sale because there's little bidding competition. But, as Grossberg learned, online consumers are still looking for bargains and often buy from the seller that *seems* to be offering the best deal. In the video game category and many other commodity categories, eBay sellers have begun offering items for greatly reduced prices, even as low as a penny. They make up the difference by charging inflated shipping and handling, sometimes as much as $20 per item. (EBay tries to discourage this practice, but it still persists.)

Grossberg grudgingly adopted this approach a year ago to stay competitive in the eBay marketplace. He maintains two separate user IDs. With one, he sells games at realistic prices with normal shipping charges. On the other ID, he discounts the games by $2, but adds a $2 shipping surcharge to keep his profit the same. Both IDs are racking up sales—the first from consumers who don't like paying inflated shipping, the second from those looking to buy at the lowest price. "EBay is constantly changing," Grossberg observes. "I have to constantly change as well to keep up and to keep selling my products. You have to constantly revisit your business model and listing practices."

When Grossberg sells items for a lower price with inflated shipping, he actually makes a bigger profit. That's because eBay charges a lower insertion fee for items that are priced below $1. The final-value fees for these lower-priced items also are less expensive.

There's actually some scientific evidence that auctions with lower opening bids but higher shipping fees produce greater profits. In 2006, two professors from the University of California at Berkeley Haas School of Business and Hong Kong University of Science and Technology posted dozens of identical CDs and Xbox video games for sale on eBay to test how consumers responded to different pricing schemes.

The initial total cost for identical items was the same, but the professors varied the opening bid price and the shipping charges to see how bidders would behave.

"In theory," the professors wrote in their study published in *Advances in Economic Analysis & Policy* (volume 6, issue 2, 2006), "dividing a price into these two pieces should have little effect on overall consumer demand for a good. A perfectly informed and fully rational consumer will merely add together the two parts of a price to obtain the total out-of-pocket price for an item and then decide whether to buy and how much to bid based on this total price."

But that's not what happened. The auctions with lower opening bid prices (and inflated shipping charges) attracted more bidders and resulted in a higher ending price and higher revenues. The professors, John Morgan of Berkeley and Tanjim Hossain of Hong Kong University, concluded that eBay shoppers may pay less attention or even completely overlook shipping costs when bidding on auctions.

Grossberg figured out a way by using those separate user IDs to sell to both those customers who ignore shipping charges when bidding and those who won't pay inflated shipping costs. In theory, that may seem as though he is competing with himself. He really isn't, though, because each consumer group has different buying preferences. Those who prefer low shipping charges are unlikely to bid on his inflated-shipping auctions, and vice versa.

As testament to his success, after 23 years with R.J. Reynolds, Grossberg quit his job in March 2005, moved his family from the northeast to Florida, and went to work full-time for 1Busyman Discount Games. He's now on his way to becoming the next online millionaire.

"It got to a point where I knew I could turn it into a full-time business," says Grossberg, who was earning a six-figure salary when he left the tobacco company and had six months earlier turned down an early retirement payout. As a full-time online entrepreneur, Grossberg has been able to maintain the same income level for himself, thanks to the million-dollar revenues he brings in every year.

"It's scary to leave a full-time job. It's extremely tough to do," he admits. "But eBay was taking up more and more of my time. I'd get up at 5 a.m. and then come in after work. Given the choice, I felt running my own business would be much better for me."

At the same time, Grossberg began exploring ways to expand his business beyond eBay through multichannel online marketing. His goal: improve profit margins and expand into as many online marketplaces as possible as a way of generating incremental sales. His first foray outside of eBay was to build his own web site at www.budget videogames.com, using ChannelAdvisor software to manage inventory and sales. So far, he can count on about 10 to 15 sales per day through the site, though that number is expected to grow significantly over time.

Grossberg markets the web site to his existing customers—people who have already purchased from him on eBay—by offering an average 10 percent discount off his eBay prices. His profit, however, remains steady because he doesn't have to pay a listing fee or final-value fee to eBay for every item that sells. Additionally, the items Grossberg has for sale on his web site are listed in the Google base directory and in Froogle, Google's shopping search engine. This allows Internet users searching for discount video games and specific titles to easily find his site.

Grossberg has also added his inventory of games to Amazon.com as part of the site's merchant program, hoping to tap into that buying audience, while increasing revenues and bolstering his brand. "What makes Amazon attractive is that it's a whole different market from eBay," Grossberg says. "There are buyers on Amazon that don't like doing business on eBay."

Unlike eBay, price is the number-one driver of sales on Amazon, according to Grossberg. Shoppers will buy from the Marketplace or Pro Merchant seller offering the lowest prices, in his experience. That's why Grossberg chose to become a Pro Merchant, instead of a basic Marketplace seller. As a Pro Merchant, he pays a monthly subscription price, but his Amazon fees and commissions are lower. Plus, he is allowed to set his own shipping and handling charges. By contrast, Amazon sets those charges automatically for Marketplace sales.

With his entire inventory listed on Amazon, Grossberg estimates that he'll eventually be able to sell an additional 50 to 100 items every day through the site with minimal work. On Amazon, instead of using PayPal or for money orders, customers must pay with a credit card when they place an order, and Amazon automatically deposits the funds into the seller's account. Unlike on eBay, customers who shop with Grossberg through Amazon don't have the option of asking him a question before buying. And once a transaction is completed, Grossberg doesn't feel obligated to leave feedback for the buyer.

"My margin will be lower," he adds. "But I'm willing to make a little bit less per game because there's a lot less work involved."

eBay Success Story

Inflatable Madness

Kevin Harmon was beginning to feel like a jinx. In the span of just a few years, he'd worked for three different technology companies in the Charlotte, North Carolina, area. All three went out of business, each time leaving Harmon unemployed.

The timing of his third layoff couldn't have happened at a worse time. Harmon found himself unemployed around Christmastime, pinching pennies as he looked for a fourth job. Hoping to satisfy his wife's Christmas wish list without breaking the bank, Harmon turned to eBay to hunt for the expensive designer purse she was expecting under the tree. There, he found much more than a bargain. Harmon, like so many others, got hooked on eBay. That online shopping trip turned into a hobby and soon thereafter a multimillion-dollar business. Now, Harmon is president of Inflatable Madness. He's on his way to becoming a bona fide online mogul with products for sale at eBay, Amazon.com, his own web site, and other Internet marketplaces.

Inflatable Madness, housed in a nondescript 3,000-square-foot warehouse in Indian Trail, a Charlotte suburb, is a Titanium Power-Seller on eBay, with $3 million in annual revenues, a number that has been growing steadily. The company sells a variety of products, including books, CDs, DVDs, and video games.

Harmon has always been able to make a living as a salesman. He worked in advertising and sales for those three failed tech companies. In college, he owned a T-shirt business. At one time, he even sold framed art on street corners. After his third layoff and before discovering eBay, he earned his income selling inflatable gorillas to car dealerships, hence the name "Inflatable Madness." While these ventures paid the bills, none were as lucrative as Harmon's growing online DVD business, which has doubled in revenues every year.

"Everything I've ever done has led up to this," says Harmon, who is married with a young child.

In the beginning, Harmon started small and in one market-place—eBay—selling off things around his house that he no longer had a use for, such as old video games, books, and movies. Those items sold surprisingly well. So, when he ran out of his own stock, Harmon began scouring for more of the same to auction off. At first, he shopped local flea markets, taking a cautious and often time-consuming approach to buying inventory. He'd visit the flea market one day to check out the available inventory and keep notes of what he found. Before buying, he'd go back home to his computer and research those items online to see what price he could get for them on eBay. If there was a profit to be made, he'd return to the flea market and buy the merchandise from the dealers. "They all hated me," Harmon recalls. "I never bought anything the first time I saw it."

This is a smart strategy. You shouldn't invest in inventory before first assessing whether there's an online market for it. Luckily, eBay makes that easy. Anyone can search recently completed auctions to determine what an item is worth on eBay. This search also provides a glimpse into the competitive atmosphere.

As Harmon's eBay sales increased, so did his buying power. Before long, those flea market vendors were happy to see him stop by their booths. Eventually, he was selling enough on eBay to begin buying from the actual suppliers, most of whom he met at trade shows and through referrals from others in the business. "All the big distributors will probably set up an account for you," Harmon says. "It's just a matter of the volume you do and the discount you receive."

Like many of his competitors, Harmon tries to offer products that aren't available through the big retail stores. He keeps his inventory deliberately broad—about 400,000 stock-keeping units (SKUs), a way of referring to individual products in inventory)—but not very deep, so he's constantly turning merchandise and making room for new music, movie, and game titles. He gets his products from a variety of sources—retailers, closeout sales, wholesalers, and distributors with overstocks. Given those diverse sources, Harmon often has to buy multiple copies of the same title. When he buys more than he can sell online, Harmon takes his pick of the best sellers and wholesales the rest. Harmon also has another way he keeps the cash flowing. He buys public domain DVDs—those that you might see in the $1 bin at Target—and sells them in lots of 100 at wholesale prices to other online sellers, since they aren't worth peddling individually.

It's getting tougher to be a smart buyer as DVD and video game retail prices drop and competition increases. In the movie and video game category, profit margins are about half what they were two years ago, Harmon says. That's because everything Inflatable Madness sells is readily available—and sometimes at a better price—from other merchants online. The key to success, Harmon says, is to sell in high volume through many marketplaces, eking out as much profit as possible on each sale. "The survivors in my category are the guys who can buy their products at the cheapest price," he says.

Given his success with the online auction site, Harmon initially was very much an eBay loyalist, putting all his effort into building his brand and clientele there. But that changed in February 2005, when the site hiked fees, making it more expensive to post auctions and sell certain items. Like many PowerSellers, Harmon chafed at the impact the fee hike would have on his business and his already-slim profit margins in a highly competitive marketplace. Instead of stewing, he channeled his anger into finding other less-expensive online marketplaces in which to sell his goods.

"Our goal is to have eBay be half of our business," says Harmon, who estimates that eBay currently accounts for 80 percent to 90 percent of the company's sales.

Harmon has good reason to look elsewhere. As someone who sells 3,000 to 4,000 items every month in a competitive category with fixed prices, he knows that fee hikes really cut into his profit margins. "A nickel truly matters," he says, especially when you multiply that nickel by 4,000 auctions a month or 48,000 auctions a year.

Harmon is not abandoning eBay, by any means. "EBay will always be an important part of our business," he insists. "They're the best at what they do. You always want to be on that site." But he is developing a strategy that will keep Inflatable Madness in business long after its growth opportunities on eBay have dissipated. Harmon projects that he can double his business on eBay before economics force him to other marketplaces, but he's wisely getting a jump start. (Some other online entrepreneurs haven't had as much foresight. Many very successful eBay companies, including a few Titanium PowerSellers who once had enviable revenues, have gone out of business after failing to evolve with the changing marketplace.)

EBay might be the single largest online marketplace, but it accounts for just 24 percent of all e-commerce activity. Armed with those numbers, Harmon decided to make a grab for a bigger piece of the online pie by listing his items for sale elsewhere, namely on eBay-owned Half.com and on Amazon.com. Unlike eBay, neither site charges upfront listing fees. Instead, they impose a commission on every sale, ranging from 5 percent to 15 percent for Half.com and from 6 percent to 15 percent, plus a 99-cent transaction fee, on Amazon.com. As another bonus, Amazon.com listings stay active for a month, cutting Harmon's workload while giving him a longer time to hook a buyer. On Half.com, listings never expire and are active until someone purchases a product or the merchant pulls it from inventory.

On its face, those fees sound high, Harmon admits. But in his business and his categories, the pricing model works because he doesn't have to pay up front to list items that might not sell. (Because of the intense competition on eBay, sell-through ratios on commodity items like DVDs can be low.) In addition, he's generally able to sell items for a bit more on Half.com and Amazon.com because the competition isn't as intense. In fact, his profit margins are higher on most items sold on these alternative sites.

As he seeks to diversify, Harmon has experimented with other auction sites, namely Overstock Auctions. With listing fees and final-value fees about half those of eBay, Overstock has successfully lured many merchants to its platform. But Overstock, which trails eBay and

Amazon in traffic, couldn't deliver the quality of customers Harmon needed. So, he ceased selling on the site. "Overstock has been a big disappointment really," he says.

Now, Harmon is focusing his efforts on building a stand-alone web site for Inflatable Madness, in hopes of driving repeat business from his existing eBay, Half.com, and Amazon customers. As one of countless sellers in these big marketplaces, Harmon has had little success in generating repeat business. In fact, only about 15 percent of Inflatable Madness' eBay business comes from repeat customers, lower than the site average. In Harmon's experience, customers are loyal to eBay and Amazon, but not to particular sellers on those platforms. Harmon hopes that having his own web site will change that because it gives him the opportunity to market directly to those who have already purchased from him.

Building a web site is often the logical next step for eBay sellers. In any retail company, repeat business is a key driver of success. But for merchants who sell in fee-based online marketplaces, there's a financial disincentive to solicit repeat business. That's because you must pay a commission for each sale, whether the customer is buying from you for the first time or the thousandth time. "We're paying eBay over and over for the same customer," says Harmon, who's not keen on sharing his profits for repeat customers.

To drive traffic to his web site, Harmon has employed a full-force marketing assault. The web site address is prominently displayed in all of his eBay auctions and store listings, as well as in Amazon.com and Half.com product listings. With each customer order, he includes a flyer with the web site address and offers special incentives to attract customers. People who buy from Inflatable Madness also have the option of opting in to the company's e-mail list. If they do, they get regular e-mail messages about new items in stock, special discounts, and sales.

In addition, Harmon lists his web site and the products for sale there in Google Base, a free service from Google. By sending a data feed with detailed descriptions of the items he's offering for sale to

Google Base, Harmon increases the chances that his inventory will show up in searches on Google and Froogle.

Although Inflatable Madness will soon open its own online real estate, Harmon has no plans to abandon his other sales channels. Selling on eBay, Amazon, and Half.com gives him tremendous exposure to millions of online shoppers. "Look at eBay as an advertising vehicle," he advises. "You want as much real estate as possible."

Remaining an active seller in multiple marketplaces also gives Inflatable Madness legitimacy. It's important to build trust among customers on these other sites first, Harmon says, and then open your own storefront after this with all the necessary security safeguards, including secure checkout and accessible customer service agents. Having a continued presence on eBay, where he has a feedback score of more than 90,000, is sure to bolster the confidence among customers discovering the Inflatable Madness online store. "We expect the web site to create synergy with our other efforts," he says.

eBay Success Story

Fleegolf

Frank Lee has found a job that combines three of his greatest loves: golf, economics, and his wife, Charlene. Together, they run the online business Fleegolf, which began in 1997.

Back then, Frank was teaching economics and serving as assistant coach of the golf team at a community college in Greenville, North Carolina. As an avid golfer, he bought, sold, and traded clubs with other golfers on the Professional Golfers' Association (PGA) web site. Through his involvement with the golf team, Frank got to know the owner of the local Pro Golf Discount store, and started selling used clubs for him online at the PGA site. When the PGA shut down its online classifieds service, Frank began selling his used clubs on eBay.

Soon thereafter, Frank's friend at Pro Golf asked for his help in selling $20,000 worth of used equipment on eBay. Suddenly, Fleegolf was on its way to becoming a real business, instead of just a sideline.

Frank's online pursuits gradually took up more of his time, and in 2003 he gave up coaching. By 2004, with the business still operating out of their home, the Lees hired their first employee. That year, they sold $110,000 worth of clubs on eBay. In 2005, Fleegolf sold just under $1 million in merchandise and Charlene retired from her job as president of the local chapter of the American Red Cross to run the company. (Frank continues to teach at the community college and plans to stay there until he is eligible for retirement. He's keeping his teaching job not out of necessity, but because he still enjoys being in the classroom, and he also doesn't want to lose his state pension and retirement benefits.) In 2006, Fleegolf's revenues reached Titanium PowerSeller status, and within several years, Frank projects the company could be doing many more millions in sales every year. "Our goal is to be the number-one golf club trade-in company in the world," he says.

The Lees plan to accomplish this with a multichannel approach that includes eBay, their own web site, search-engine optimization, and a presence on comparison-shopping engines. Branding has become very important for Fleegolf in its quest to become the biggest golf club trade-in company in the world. Every item is shipped in a branded Fleegolf box, and customers receive free gifts with every purchase—usually tees, ink pens, and can covers emblazoned with the company logo and web site address. The Lees also enclose standard package inserts with every shipment, including a business card and instructions on how golfers can trade in used and unwanted clubs for cash.

In their business, the Lees concentrate on previously owned golf clubs that have been traded in at stores or through the company's web site. Their average selling price on eBay ranges from $71 to $105 because they deal mostly in expensive golf clubs. But they also sell a variety of golf accessories—head covers, grips, key chains, towels, gloves, visors, and wristbands—that they purchase at closeout from golf shops that have gone out of business, as well as golf apparel purchased directly from manufacturers.

They have agreements to buy trade-in equipment from many Pro Golf franchisees; Copeland Sports, a chain of sporting goods stores in California, Nevada, Oregon, and Utah; and Martin's Golf and Tennis in Myrtle Beach, South Carolina, as well as other stores. Frank publishes a new price list every month that indicates what the company will pay for hundreds of different clubs. Stores use this price list to set their own trade-in rates, and they send the used equipment to Fleegolf's North Carolina warehouse for reimbursement. The Lees sell the trade-in merchandise on eBay (in both auctions and the Fleegolf eBay store), and on their own web site.

Fleegolf receives daily shipments of clubs from its suppliers, as well as from individuals who trade in their clubs on the Fleegolf web site (www.fleegolf.com). Every item is cleaned and graded, according to a 10-point scale that Frank devised. Fleegolf sells only clubs that score 7.0 or better. A 7.0-rated club is structurally sound but shows heavy wear with numerous scratches, marks, rock dings, and bag wear on the shaft. By contrast, a 9.9-rated club is deemed to be in mint condition, still wrapped in its original plastic. The majority of the clubs Fleegolf sells fall somewhere between the two extremes. They likely show signs of normal to moderate use and slight cosmetic defects, but are still course-worthy.

Though many of Fleegolf's competitors use stock photography on their web sites and eBay ads, Frank insists that each item Fleegolf sells be photographed by his employees. In fact, every product listing includes multiple photographs of the item to emphasize its condition. Each club is photographed from at least three different angles so customers can see for themselves what condition it is in. (Employees take five photographs of putters and six to seven photographs of iron sets.) The photographs, in conjunction with Fleegolf's condition rating scale, allow shoppers to make informed buying decisions, Frank says. And because they're seeing the item from every possible vantage point, they're less likely to be disappointed when they receive it.

"From the beginning, Frank always talked about the online pro shop," says Chad Foster, Fleegolf's first employee and one of Frank's former students. The idea, Foster explains, is to recreate the pro shop shopping experience online so that customers feel like they are actually holding the clubs in their hands. "If you can describe an item and do the pictures well enough, it's like they've seen it in person and you are therefore more likely to sell it," he says.

After each club is rated and photographed, it is then tagged with a unique bar code, which helps with inventory management and prevents shipping errors in Fleegolf's warehouse. When an item is posted for sale on eBay or on the company's web site, that bar code is scanned. When a club is shelved, an employee scans the bar code on the club and on the shelf so it can be easily retrieved. Before a shipment goes out, the bar code is scanned again to make sure the club has been included in the right order. The scanning software integrates with Fleegolf's inventory and auction management software from Kyozou.com so an item is immediately taken out of inventory once it sells, preventing listing mistakes.

Buying the scanners and Kyozou's multichannel sales automation software has been one of the best decisions the Lees have made during their 10 years in business. Specifically, they were able to scale their business and streamline operations after computerizing everything. Imagine this: Before they started using Kyozou and the scanners, the Lees would tag each club by hand and copy down the eBay item number when they posted it for sale. If an item failed to sell on the first try, they'd mark through the old eBay item number and write down the new digits. Some clubs, which have remained in inventory for a while, still wear their old manila tags with many item numbers scratched out.

What's more, the software enables Frank to more closely monitor his spending on eBay—which totals about $10,000 a month in fees. He uses this data, combined with his expertise as an economist and statistician, to determine the most profitable course of action when it comes to listing items for auction on eBay, in his eBay store, or on the Fleegolf web site.

The software and Marketplace Research data on eBay allows Frank to analyze the profit margin on each category of items he sells and choose the best marketplace based on those results. He often uses historical sales results from auctions, for example, to determine how high to set Buy It Now prices and to figure out what to charge on his eBay store and Fleegolf's web site. He also uses the data to predict seasonality trends. Demand for golf clubs and related products begins to increase in March and peaks when the weather warms and the major professional tournaments are under way. At these times of year, Frank is likely to charge more for merchandise, no matter where or in what format he's selling it, because consumer demand supports the higher pricing. On eBay, he's more likely to run more auctions during the peak March-to-June season rather than selling things at fixed prices. "If it's something we think people will fight over, we don't use a Buy It Now price," he says. For these same reasons, Fleegolf concentrates most of its comparison-shopping engine spending during this four-month period when demand for golf products is highest.

Data has also helped Frank pinpoint the item that has the best profit potential. As a result, he is now seeking to buy and sell more iron sets and supplement those sales with complementary items. Less expensive items, like golf club head covers, deliver a higher profit margin (71 percent), but they bring in only about $15,000 in revenues every year. By comparison, Fleegolf's gross profit margin on iron sets is 36 percent on revenues of several hundred thousand dollars annually. (Driver sales account for an almost equal amount of revenues, but they're just a tad less profitable.)

As profitability increases, Frank plans to expand Fleegolf's multi-channel reach. Buying keywords on Google and other search engines and driving paid traffic to his web site and eBay listings is next on his agenda. "We think by going into these other channels, it might help our revenues," Frank says. "More people will find exactly what they want."

Cost control is definitely the name of the game at Fleegolf. The Lees are particularly cognizant of inefficiencies that might cost them money. Take warehousing, for example. Ten years into the business, the Lees are operating out of their third office warehouse. (Their first was their garage—then later every spare space in their house.) About two years ago, they purchased a condo in a business park, figuring it could serve as both their warehouse and office for several years. But the business outgrew that space in two months' time, so the Lees moved into a 3,500-square-foot facility in the same business park. Their goal is to keep overhead steady and stay there for at least several more years. How can they accomplish this at a time when their inventory is growing along with sales? By turning merchandise quickly—Frank's ultimate goal is weekly—and with smart space and inventory management techniques.

Once they've been photographed and posted online, golf clubs are racked side-by-side on unique wooden storage units that Frank designed. Each unit, which stands about seven feet tall, contains several four-inch-tall shelves stacked perpendicularly to each other so golf clubs can be stored front to back and side to side. Each shelf can accommodate about 15 clubs and provides the perfect solution for "getting the most clubs in the smallest possible space," Charlene says. Not only do the shelves save space, but they also save time that the Lees and their employees once spent hunting for merchandise scattered here and there. In this business, time and space equal money.

Frank knows that many of Fleegolf's competitors store golf clubs in boxes so they're ready for shipment. But in his mind, that's an inefficient use of space, particularly in view of the fact that many customers order multiple items. If Fleegolf employees boxed items in advance, they'd waste time after a sale pulling clubs from boxes and consolidating them into another package for shipment. (Although the Lees don't prebox golf clubs, they do put smaller items, such as T-shirts, tees, and coffee mugs, in the packaging that they'll be shipped in. This prevents such items from being lost or misplaced, Charlene notes.)

The Lees also employ space-saving techniques in their shipping department. They use boxes that are sized to fit the particular club that they're shipping rather than standard 4-foot-by-4-inch-by-4-inch cardboard boxes. The idea is to eliminate wasted space and save on shipping costs, which is particularly important for a company like Fleegolf that charges a flat-rate shipping fee. (Many delivery companies, in addition to charging for the weight of an item, figure the box's dimensions into the cost. A bigger box costs more to ship.)

Ultimately, these strategies help Fleegolf's bottom line and explain how a garage venture has grown into a multimillion-dollar business in just a few years.

2

Conquering Amazon

The Lowdown

Amazon.com is now one of the Web's biggest retailers. In 1994, however, it was just an entrepreneur's fledgling dream. Founder Jeff Bezos had an idea that the Internet could offer book lovers a unique experience they couldn't have in any traditional bookstore—the ability to browse a selection of millions of titles in a single sitting. In July 1995, Bezos began selling books online from his Seattle garage, fulfilling orders for customers in 50 states and 45 countries in that first month alone. Now, the company's sales total more than $8.4 billion annually.

In the 12 years since, Amazon.com has evolved into much more than an online bookstore. Now, the company is one of the best-known brands on the Web. It offers a virtual smorgasbord of anything people want to buy online—books, movies, music, gourmet food, computers, clothing, electronics, drugstore items, cameras, sporting goods, tools, hardware, and the list goes on. The company is well on its way to achieving Bezos' ultimate goal of offering the "Earth's biggest selection." Part of the way Amazon has achieved this is through partnering with other companies—including Toys " Я " Us,

Target, and Borders—and by opening its marketplace to other merchants of all types and sizes.

In 1999, Amazon launched its own auction platform, as well as an initiative called zShops that enabled individuals and large merchants to open stores and list products for sale for a low monthly subscription fee and a cut of revenues. A year later, Amazon further opened itself to outside sellers with the creation of its Marketplace program. Anyone with something to sell—be it new or used—can be an Amazon Marketplace seller. There are no monthly subscription fees and no upfront listing fees. Charges are levied only when an Amazon Marketplace item is sold. Now, Amazon also has what it calls "Pro Merchants," mostly medium-sized to large sellers whose products are included in the general Amazon catalog. These Pro Merchants typically list and sell a large volume of goods on the site every month, thus supplementing their own website sales. Third-party sales on Amazon .com have grown significantly since the programs started in 2000. Once accounting for just 6 percent of items sold on the web site, merchandise from third-party merchants now amounts to almost 30 percent of Amazon's sales.

There's yet another way for outsiders to make money on Amazon. The e-tailer has operated its Associates program since 1996 and essentially created the model for online affiliate marketing programs. Today, Amazon's is the largest and most successful online affiliate program with more one million members worldwide. Affiliates earn between 4 percent and 10 percent in referral fees for promoting Amazon products on their own sites.

Jeff Bezos, in realizing his own dream of online entrepreneurial success, has helped thousands of others achieve theirs by opening Amazon.com to third-party transactions. The site, which continues to grow in popularity every year, is a good channel for growing incremental sales. Many merchants flock to Amazon because of its huge audience and buyer- and seller-friendly policies. Though it's a more expensive marketplace by comparison, sellers report that they encounter less fraud and fewer customer service hassles from Amazon buyers while spending less on managing sales in this channel than in others.

Getting Started

In order to sell on Amazon.com, you'll need to create an account. (If you're already a customer, there's no need to register a separate account, although Amazon does recommend that you maintain separate ones for personal purchases and business sales.)

When you sell at Amazon, the company collects all payments and distributes them to you via a bank draft every two weeks. Therefore, it is important to register for Amazon Payments. You'll choose a nickname for your company—similar to your user ID on eBay—and will also be asked to provide your phone number and checking account information (including account numbers and routing numbers) so you can get paid for what you sell.

If you're a new seller, you'll have to wait at least 14 days before receiving any cash from Amazon for sales completed through this web site. This is purely a security measure that gives Amazon time to make sure you abide by its seller requirements and don't welsh on any transactions. After this two-week holding period, you can manually disburse funds to your checking account daily, if you choose.

Finally, before you start listing products on the site, you'll need to set up your seller preferences, in which you outline your default shipping method, as well as your customer service and returns policies.

With these steps completed, you're set to begin listing individual items for sale in the Amazon Marketplace. In order to outfit your own zShops storefront or easily sell in volume, you'll need a Pro Merchant subscription, which will enable you to upload listings in bulk. You'll pay $19.99 a month for your first two months as a Pro Merchant subscriber and $39.99 a month thereafter. (You must register a credit card with Amazon for monthly subscription charges.)

For the cost, Pro Merchants get privileges that other Marketplace sellers don't, along with discounted selling fees. Pro Merchants have the ability to list an unlimited number of products for sale on Amazon every month, and can open a zShops storefront that can be promoted directly to customers, something basic Marketplace sellers can't do. Basic Marketplace listings expire after 60 days, but Pro Merchant listings stay active until the item sells. In addition, Amazon charges Pro Merchants less for every sale they make through the site. Most Marketplace sellers pay a 99-cent transaction fee on every sale, plus a commission of 6 percent to 15 percent. Amazon automatically waives the 99-cent transaction fee for Pro Merchant subscribers.

The next step to selling on Amazon is actually listing your products for sale. I'll first walk you the process that a basic Marketplace seller would use, and then tell you about the bulk-listing tools available to Pro Merchant subscribers.

The great thing about Amazon is that most of the products you'll want to sell are probably already cataloged on the web site. So, setting up a listing is really simple. From any Amazon product detail page, you just click on the link to "Sell yours here." You'll have the option of grading your item as new, refurbished, used, or collectible and adding a comment about the item's condition. Next, you'll set the price for your product, based on your own inventory cost and what Amazon and other Marketplace sellers charge for the same product. Finally, you'll choose your shipping options—standard, international, or expedited—and submit your listing for inclusion in the Amazon.com search database. Before submitting the listing, you'll get a chance to review it and to see how much you'll earn, minus Amazon's commissions, if the item sells.

As a Pro Merchant subscriber, you'll probably find it much easier to submit multiple product listings at once, using management software like Monsoon, SellerEngine, ChannelAdvisor, or the site's free Inventory Loader tool. If you use Inventory Loader, you'll need to aggregate your inventory database into a single tab-delimited text file, which is essentially a spreadsheet file saved in a specific format that Amazon can read. Your spreadsheet must include specific fields, such as the item's International Standard Book Number (ISBN) or Universal Product Code (UPC), price, and quantity available, in a specific order. To ensure that your bulk upload file includes all the information Amazon requires, download the spreadsheet template at www.amazon.com/exec/obidos/tg/browse/-/1161314/ref=br_bx_c_ 1_0/103-7307034-5587808 and fill in all the necessary information for your products. You may find it necessary to make revisions to your Amazon inventory as you sell stock on other web sites or add new items to your product catalog, and you can do so by submitting modifications and additions through a separate bulk upload file.

Occasionally, you may want to sell an item that's not already included in Amazon's vast product catalog. Pro Merchant subscribers have the option of adding what Amazon calls "product detail pages" in 15 categories—baby; books; camera and photo; computer and video games; electronics; kitchen, home, and garden; music; musical instruments; pet supplies; software; sporting goods; tools and hardware; toys and games; video and DVD; and everything else. Catalog additions cannot be made to the following Amazon categories, also known as stores: apparel and accessories; beauty; cell phones and cell phone plans; gourmet food; jewelry and watches; magazines; office products; and health and personal care.

Once you've determined that a product you want to sell isn't already included in the Amazon catalog, you can begin the manual process of creating a product detail page. First, you'll classify the product by category, subcategory, and type with prompting at each stage by Amazon. Next, you'll add the product details—specifically the product name, manufacturer, or publisher—and a description that will appear in the online catalog. It's important to note that the description should be a basic one, without specific information about the condition of the item you're offering for sale. That's because the description will be used by you as well as other merchants who sell the product on Amazon in the future.

After submitting your product details, Amazon evaluates the listing. If you've done everything correctly, the item will be added to the site's product catalog immediately. You will have the option of adding up to eight images to your product submission, provided those photographs meet Amazon's criteria. Preferably, products should be photographed against a white background, and they must be in focus and well lit. Image files can be no larger than 50 kilobytes in size and at least 500 pixels in length to be properly displayed. Once a product is accepted into Amazon's catalog, you can start selling the item, following the steps outlined earlier in this chapter.

How It Works

The great thing about Amazon is that your listings appear alongside those offered by the e-tailer itself and its large merchant partners, like Target, Office Depot, and The Bombay Company. Shoppers can choose to buy directly from Amazon, from one of its big retail partners, or from smaller merchants like you. Price is often the determining factor.

Take, for instance, a search for "Sony PlayStation Portable," a popular, handheld video game system. The main product page lists a unit available for $199.99 directly from Amazon.com, but shoppers also have the opportunity to choose from "24 new and used" game systems offered at various prices by third-party sellers on Amazon. These listings are grouped by condition and then by ascending price. Shoppers can see at a glance how the various third-party merchants rank in terms of customer satisfaction and service thanks to Amazon's five-star seller rating system.

Customers interested only in items from third-party sellers also have the option of just browsing or searching zShops listings. Or they can visit a zShops seller's storefront directly to see everything that merchant has to offer.

Although it is competing with these third-party merchants, Amazon makes it safe and easy for customers to buy from Marketplace sellers by extending its product and security guarantees to those transactions. Amazon processes all financial transactions conducted on its web site, meaning that buyers never have to share their credit card information with unfamiliar sellers. When customers decide to buy a product from an Amazon Marketplace seller, they complete the checkout process as if they were buying directly from Amazon. Amazon then sends an e-mail receipt to the buyer and another e-mail notifying the seller that a particular item has sold. That seller e-mail includes instructions for shipping the product to the buyer, but doesn't contain any of the buyer's private credit card information. Amazon pays sellers every two weeks with automated direct deposits to their bank accounts.

A big difference between Amazon and the other online marketplaces is its relatively simple fee structure. Sellers pay no listing fees—only commissions after a sale. As previously mentioned, basic Marketplace sellers pay a commission plus a 99-cent transaction fee for every sale, which is waived for Pro Merchant subscribers. Expect to pay a 15 percent commission on most items sold at Amazon.com, with a few notable exceptions. The commission rate is 6 percent on computers; 8 percent on cameras, photo equipment, and electronics; and 10 percent on items in Amazon's Everything Else store.

Unlike other online marketplaces, you have little control over shipping charges and policies. Amazon requires that third-party merchants ship products within two business days of receiving a customer's order. When you sell an item in the Amazon Marketplace, Amazon gives you a shipping credit to help cover your costs. The actual amount of the credit depends on the type of product you're selling—the credit for books, video games, and DVDs ranges from $2.49 to $3.49—which should cover the cost of shipping a two- or three-pound item with the U.S. Postal Service via media mail. The standard shipping credit for other items is a flat $4.49, plus 50 cents per pound. As a seller, you're obligated to ship the item even if the credit doesn't cover your costs. So, make sure to account for additional shipping, packaging, and handling fees when setting your selling price on Amazon.

Like most marketplaces, Amazon has a feedback system through which buyers can rate third-party merchants. Interestingly, however, many Amazon sellers don't put as much emphasis on cultivating high feedback scores as they do on sites like eBay. That may be because the Amazon Marketplace already provides buyers with an added level of confidence and security because of the financial protections that are in place.

Amazon also takes steps to monitor sellers' performance and measure them against specific category benchmarks. From your seller account page within Amazon, you can access your "Performance Summary" for all past transactions. The summary provides a consolidated view of sales, refunds, feedback, and any claims customers have made against you. Amazon sets performance targets for sellers in each category. Those sellers identified as poor performers will receive an e-mail from Amazon with tips on how to improve their performance ratings.

What Sells Best

You'll find just about everything under the sun for sale at Amazon. That opens up a wealth of opportunities for third-party merchants to sell in one of 34 different categories, from books to toys and games. Your success as a seller is directly tied to your ability to offer those items that Amazon shoppers are searching for. You can download a Google Desktop gadget at http://desktop.google.com/plugins/i/amazontop.html that will give you the running totals of the best sellers in each category. You may be able to use that data for your own inventory planning purposes.

Not surprisingly, given Amazon's roots as an online bookstore, media categories (books, movies, music, DVDs, video games, and computer software) represent the lion's share of the company's revenues, with electronics and other goods accounting for the remaining third. Amazon is a particularly good supplementary channel for online media sellers because it delivers customers searching for precisely those products. Third-party sellers may find it difficult to compete with Amazon's prices on new books, music, and movies. But, much more so than eBay's Half.com, the site has proven to be a great place to sell used products in these categories.

Amazon offers sellers of books, music, videos, and DVDs an interesting option for promoting their products by piggybacking on popular product searches. Sellers in these categories may cross-link their items with others in the Amazon.com catalog. For example, a merchant selling a book about *Star Wars* could cross-link that item with the DVD of *Return of the Jedi* and a *Star Wars* video game. By doing so, you ensure that the book is also promoted on the product detail pages of those other items. Sellers who cross-link their listings sell at a rate 20 percent higher than those who do not, according to Amazon. (Two things to remember: Amazon limits cross-linking to products within the books, music, video, and DVD stores. And items in the top 500 in any Amazon.com store are not eligible for cross-links.)

In electronics, audio and video, camera and photo, and similar categories, many sellers are finding success with refurbished products. These items, which have been rebuilt by the manufacturer or certified technicians, are generally priced significantly lower than identical brand-new products. Consumers aren't as fearful of purchasing refurbished electronics products as they are of purchasing used ones. Refurbished products often carry a warranty and money-back guarantee, and they are generally considered to be as good as new items in functionality, if not in cosmetic appearance.

Another way to improve your chances of success on Amazon is by selling in niche categories, focusing on popularly searched for items that aren't widely available from other sellers. You'll find that Amazon can be a price-motivated marketplace, though perhaps less so than eBay or the comparison-shopping engines. Your products will be listed alongside those offered by Amazon.com and other third-party sellers. All other things being equal, sellers offering the lowest price are most likely to catch the buyer. However, Amazon customers tend to be swayed by other factors, such as the third-party seller's brand reputation, customer-service policies, seller rating, and record of positive transactions.

Another smart strategy on Amazon.com is to time your listings to coincide with peak traffic times. As is the case for any retailer, Amazon's sales peak is in the fourth quarter of the year when consumers turn to the Internet for their holiday shopping. Depending on the category, it's not unusual for an Amazon merchant's sales to triple or quadruple in the final quarter of the year because of the increased holiday traffic to the web site. To take advantage of this phenomenon, some merchants boost their Amazon inventory toward the end of the year and add items that would make good gifts to their product offerings.

Pros and Cons

Ask Amazon sellers what they like best about the marketplace, and they're likely to mention that it's fairly hassle free to sell there. Sellers don't have to pay exorbitant listing fees. They don't have to answer questions from prospective buyers. They don't have to photograph items for sale or write detailed descriptions. They don't have to collect payments. They don't have to deal with bidder and buyer fraud. They don't have to relist items that don't sell.

Yet, for all these pluses, there are some drawbacks to selling on Amazon. Most importantly, the site charges pretty high commissions, perhaps to account for the no-listing-fees model. In most product categories, the commission rate is 15 percent. You'll need to figure that into your asking price to ensure that you earn a profit on sales. Although Amazon pays you a shipping credit for every item as well, you'll need to make sure that's enough to cover your actual shipping costs, including postage and product packaging. If not, adjust your asking price upward.

Unfortunately, Amazon does not allow its third-party merchants to undercut Marketplace prices on their own web sites. If you're selling a product for $20 at Amazon (excluding shipping), you can't charge less for it on your own site or the listing will be yanked. When he began selling at Amazon.com, Dave Reeder of Captain Dave's Survival Center and Army Navy Supply found that he needed to raise his prices across the board in order to be profitable. In his case, the move paid off, and Amazon now delivers a good portion of his million dollars in annual sales. (You'll read more about how Reeder does it in a moment.)

Here's another important thing to remember about this particular online sales channel: You'll be competing directly with Amazon, one of the Web's biggest retailers, as well as with thousands of other merchants just like yourself. This could prove to be an advantage if you're able to offer better prices and service than your competitors. However, you may also feel the squeeze when it comes to pricing, particularly for new items. A big company like Amazon has tremendous buying power and buckets of money to spend on marketing and promotions, meaning that it can sell some products for less than you can purchase them at wholesale. You stand a much better chance of succeeding in this channel if you don't compete head-to-head with Amazon in its primary merchandise categories—books, movies, and music—and instead focus on underserved niches or used product categories.

Action Plan

Here's how to get up and running as a merchant on Amazon.com:

✔ Register for an Amazon seller account, keeping in mind that you may employ the same user ID and password you use when buying on Amazon.com.

✔ Sign up for Amazon Payments by providing a valid checking account where you can receive biweekly direct deposits from Amazon.com.

✔ Experiment as a basic Marketplace seller first by listing used books, movies, and CDs for sale on Amazon. The easiest way to get a feel for how the process works is to sell your past purchases from the Amazon "Sell Your Stuff" main page. Follow Amazon's pricing guidelines and see what competitors are charging to determine how much to sell your items for.

✔ Calculate how many items you expect to sell every month on Amazon.com. Multiply that number by $0.99. You'll pay at least that much in transaction fees unless you have a volume selling account with the site.

✔ If you plan to list a lot of items for sale on Amazon.com, sign up for a Pro Merchant subscription, which costs $39.99 monthly but will save you 99 cents on every transaction.

✔ Prepare your product listings for Amazon, using third-party inventory management software or the site's Inventory Loader tool. Be sure to include specifics such as the product identification number (usually an ISBN or UPC number), the quantity available, the item condition, and your asking price.

✔ Monitor competing listings to make sure your prices are competitive with those of Amazon.com and other merchants. Whenever possible, strive to offer the product at the lowest possible price.

✔ Negotiate volume discounts with shipping companies to ensure that your delivery costs are covered by the shipping allowance Amazon gives you for every item.

✔ In categories where it's allowed, cross-link your items to give them additional exposure on Amazon.com.

✔ If you're a Pro Merchant subscriber, create a zShops storefront where customers can come to see all items you have in inventory. Include the URL for your zShops store in all your marketing materials and communications with customers who find you through Amazon and other online channels.

Amazon.com Success Story

Djangos

As the new president of Gottschalks, a California-based regional department store chain, Steve Furst was tasked with trimming the company's expenses. One way to do this, he proposed, was by building a web site. For one thing, by posting its quarterly financials online instead of mailing out statements, Furst determined that Gottschalks could save $60,000 annually. At the same time, the site would position the department store for future growth. So, Furst took his idea to the board of directors.

"You realize, Steve," the chairman bluntly asserted, "that this [the Web] is nothing more than a trend, like CB radios and eight-track tapes."

Furst fired back with his own frank assessment. "I didn't present this for a vote because none of you are qualified to make this decision," he responded. "None of you understand the future of what we're going to do."

Thus begins the story of how Steve Furst, a career department store executive, became an online entrepreneur. The tale has taken quite a few twists and turns during the past 14 years as Furst hopscotched from the department store to a Web consulting company and then a fledgling dot-com. But more on all that later. Let's first turn back to Gottschalks to see just how Furst proved that the board chairman was wrong about the Internet.

Despite the board's trepidation, Furst proceeded with his plan to build a web site for Gottschalks. He recruited students from a local college to program, host, and maintain it. Initially, the site was little more than a repository for the company's quarterly reports and other investor relations information. Soon enough, though, Furst decided that he also could use the Web to sell products. He convened a meeting of the company's merchandise buyers, showed them a digital camera, and asked them to bring him their best items to feature on the Internet. One of the buyers suggested that Gottschalks use the Web to sell a new line of neckties and scarves designed by Rush Limbaugh's then-wife. Furst agreed, and even convinced Limbaugh to promote the Gottschalks web site on his nationally syndicated radio talk show. Sales of the ties and scarves, which weren't available in many other outlets, took off. "We were getting orders for $800 worth of ties," Furst reveals, reliving the thrill of getting in on the ground floor of e-commerce and the vindication he felt at proving the chairman of the board wrong.

And how wrong the chairman was, both in dismissing the Internet as a fad and in discounting Furst's idea for using it to strengthen Gottschalks' financial position.

Furst is now proving just how right he was about the Internet as the president of Djangos.com, a multimillion-dollar online retailer that ships out thousands of used CDs every day to customers around the world. The company sells through its own web site, a European web site, Amazon.com, Half.com, Alibris.com, and other Internet portals where people go to buy music.

Djangos didn't begin as an Internet retailer. In fact, far from it. In 1973, Bob Dietsche opened Django Record Company, a dingy record store named for legendary jazz guitarist Django Reinhardt, in downtown Portland, Oregon. Twenty-six years later, new owners purchased the store and changed its name to Djangos. The new owners planned to buy dozens of other independent record stores throughout the country and sell their inventory online through a web site at www.djangos.com.

Things worked well for a while, but it soon became clear that the new owners' business model was at least partially flawed. Buying independent record stores left the company in debt, and in 2002, Djangos filed for Chapter 11 bankruptcy protection. "They spent $14 million buying old beat-up record stores, and almost all of them are out of business," Furst says.

That's when Furst and his two business partners, Donie Treadaway and Alan Brown, stepped in. They ditched the company's plans to buy up more record stores and instead focused on growing Djangos' online presence. They rewrote the software they used to list products from the company's surviving bricks-and-mortar stores online and began allowing other independent music retailers to use it in return for a 15 percent cut on every sale. "We went to these small stores that were struggling to survive and Web-enabled them," Furst says.

Now, more than 458 local record stores sell under the Djangos banner through the company's own web site and its stores on Amazon and various other online channels. Djangos, the corporate entity, also maintains a 10,000-square-foot facility in Portland where it ware-houses half a million CDs—most of them on consignment from stores that have gone out of business—and receives just-in-time inventory shipments from the nation's three biggest new music distributors.

But it is Djangos' relationship with independent music stores that makes it such a sales juggernaut. Twice a day, stores upload their in-ventory to the Djangos server, which aggregates the offerings from hundreds of independent retailers into a single catalog comprising millions of new and used CDs, movies, and video games. Djangos con-tinuously updates its Web catalog and listings in other online market-places to keep them current. Customers place their orders directly with Djangos, either through the company's web site or on one of the other online marketplaces, and the independent stores handle fulfillment.

By incorporating the independent retailers' merchandise with its own, Djangos can offer its customers a much wider product selection but without having to buy any inventory or pay to warehouse it. The independent music stores benefit from the partnership as well because the Web greatly expands their customer base and provides them with a more profitable alternative sales channel.

"There is a market for out-of-print music that people love," Furst says. "The typical music store has a 10-mile radius customer base." The Internet expands that exponentially, and at the same time enables mu-sic merchants to sell their products for higher prices than the local market would support. Stores that sell online through Djangos can earn margins as high as 60 percent for CDs they've bought from trade-in customers, numbers that are impossible to achieve through in-store-only sales, Furst says.

Djangos processes all payments and orders, whether they come through the company's e-commerce site or another online channel. The company then farms the orders out to the independent retailers, who are supposed to ship them the next day. Customers may receive multiple shipments from Djangos, depending on where the items within their order are stocked. One CD might ship from a store in California, another might ship from a store in South Carolina, and yet another from the Djangos warehouse in Oregon. Despite having all these far-flung distribution depots, Djangos has low shipping fees, products reach customers quickly, and quality control is rarely an issue. The company truly is a study in logistics efficiency and supremacy.

Just how does Djangos accomplish this? First off, the company has strict guidelines for its merchant partners. Stores are required to ship orders the morning after receipt, and Djangos uses its software to keep tabs on this performance. If stores fall behind on fulfillment or get swamped with orders, Djangos yanks their products from its inventory database so they're no longer visible to Web shoppers.

"They know we're monitoring them," Furst says, noting that stores also are held financially responsible for any order-processing mistakes they make. Djangos pays for the return shipment of any damaged or below-standard products and gives the customer a credit, which is charged back to the offending store. "If they were negligent in any way that we can determine, they'll pay for the whole thing to take care of the customer. Our creed is that they're going to make you happy."

Instead of sending products out media mail via the U.S. Postal Service, Djangos and its merchant partners use DHL's SmartMail service. SmartMail is what's known as an inserter into the postal service. When you drop off a package at the local post office, it travels to a series of postal service sorting facilities throughout the country before arriving at the final recipient. Djangos packages skip those steps in the middle. Instead, its packages are sent to a central DHL facility where they're sorted, then inserted deep into the U.S. Postal Service mail stream for delivery to the recipient. That ensures faster delivery. Because it is a volume shipper, Djangos has negotiated shipping rates with DHL that are about one-third of what the delivery company normally charges. This means customers aren't penalized if they order items that must be shipped from multiple Djangos network stores. Djangos charges a flat $1 handling fee for every order, plus 99 cents for each item for standard delivery domestic orders. (International shipping doesn't cost much more—just $1.99 per item, plus a $2 handling fee per order.) Djangos also negotiates bulk shipping supply discounts, so most networked stores have an incentive to use approved packaging. Most Djangos items ship out in padded envelopes that cost 11.5 cents, much less than the market rate.

Again, all these methods keep shipping costs low, which allows Djangos to easily sell into international markets, something many online companies struggle with. From its American web site, found at www.djangos.com, the company ships to an estimated 210 foreign countries every day and that number is projected to increase exponentially as Djangos signs more foreign-based record stores to sell on its European site, www.djangos.eu. In fact, international sales are about half of Djangos.com's business and most of that is fueled by items sold directly from the company's web site and through its Amazon zShops store at www.amazon.com/shops/djangomusic. Djangos was once a major seller on Half.com, as well. While the company still sells there, it has deemphasized that channel because Half.com doesn't accept orders from international buyers.

As for its marketing efforts, Djangos relies heavily on existing customers for repeat business and word-of-mouth advertising. The Djangos "HighNotes" newsletter is e-mailed to more than a million customers several times a month. It includes, among other things, discounts and exclusive offers available only to newsletter subscribers. Customers also have the option of compiling a wish list of CDs they want to buy. When Djangos gets the titles in stock, it notifies the customer and that usually results in a sale. The company also has affiliates that post Djangos banner ads on their web sites and earn a 5 percent commission for every sale they push to the site.

Customers can also earn easy rewards for referring their friends to Djangos.com. "It's guerrilla marketing at its finest," Furst insists, and it's one of the ways the company has been able to grow so fast.

Amazon.com Success Story

Captain Dave's

Dave Reeder isn't what you would expect of a survivalist. He lives in a house in the suburbs, not a cabin in the woods. And he dresses in khakis and dress shirts, not camouflage and combat boots. If you met Reeder, you'd probably think he worked in an important position for some big corporation. And all of that used to be true. But now Reeder is the proprietor of a million-dollar Internet business, Captain Dave's Survival Center and Army Navy Supply.

Reeder's path to online entrepreneurship began in 1995 when he was working at a public relations agency in Pittsburgh. Reeder was the most tech-savvy guy in the agency—but that wasn't saying much because he was no computer guru. Still, Reeder's boss dragged him along on a pitch meeting with an Internet service provider (ISP). The agency didn't get the ISP's business, but Reeder left that meeting with a sign-up disk for the Internet service and an inkling that he'd stumbled onto something big. He immediately signed up for an account with the ISP and started tinkering on the Internet. Reeder, always a closet survivalist, decided to teach himself HTML coding and put up a web site with tips on long-term food storage, survival medicine, and other similar topics. He mined Listservs and newsgroups for his content for www.survival-center.com. To say the site took off was an understatement. Reeder was soon getting so much traffic on the discussion forums on his site that he was using up his allotted bandwidth. He started charging users a few bucks a month to participate in the forums and used the cash to purchase more bandwidth to keep the site active.

Pretty soon, as the site grew in popularity, visitors started asking Reeder to send them his catalog. He didn't have one, "but it didn't take too many people asking for my catalog for me to start thinking about selling products," Reeder says. He responded to an ad in the back of *American Survival Guide* magazine and became a distributor for Ready Reserve long-term storage food. Aside from a $50 signup fee, Reeder didn't have to invest another dime with Ready Reserve. He simply listed the products on his web site for about 20 percent above wholesale. When something sold, Reeder forwarded the order to Ready Reserve, which would drop ship the products to his customers. At the end of every month, Ready Reserve cut Reeder a check for his sales, minus his wholesale costs. "The first month, I got an $800 check," he says.

Reeder couldn't have picked a better time to go into the survival business. Operating from a new site, www.captaindaves.com, he made his first online sale in 1998, around the same time fears about Y2K began ramping up. "I was selling thousands and thousands of dollars' worth of food a month," says Reeder, who by that time was working in the corporate communications department of a big company. "Every day, I was coming home from my real job, processing orders, and faxing them out to Ready Reserve a couple of times a week."

Then, as had happened before, Reeder's customers began asking for products he didn't have. So, he sought out other suppliers, this time buying inventory outright with profits from his past online sales. "I started warehousing water filters and MREs," the prepackaged ready-to-eat meals that the military serves to troops. "I'd get a pallet of MREs delivered to my house and unpack them to my basement."

These items sold well and quickly until the clock struck midnight on January 1, 2000, and people worldwide realized that Y2K was more hype than real threat. Some of Reeder's suppliers even went out of business, and his own online sales leveled off.

Then the terrorist attacks of September 2001 happened, followed quickly by anthrax scares, heightened fears of bioterrorism, and the United States' military involvement in Afghanistan and Iraq. More Americans started worrying about their safety in uncertain times, and Reeder's business once again picked up. "There was an interest in [storage] food, and we started selling gas masks," he says. "People wanted to buy rafts so that they could paddle across the Hudson River and get out of New York City."

Though he was admittedly pleased with the upturn his business had taken, Reeder knew that he couldn't keep riding the coattails of fear if he wanted to stay in business. "It became evident that this was a very cyclical business and that I needed to do something to even it out," he says. Reeder, knowing his customer base as well as he did, convinced Rothco, a large army-navy supplier, to let him sell its clothing and other products on his web site.

Selling apparel on the Web is difficult and it can be costly because of the inventory investment necessary. You can't offer a camouflage T-shirt in just one size; you have to offer it in a range of sizes. Initially, Reeder didn't want the burden of warehousing that much inventory, so he'd buy from Rothco only when he had enough online orders to satisfy the company's $200 wholesale order requirement.

Soon after, Amazon.com approached Reeder with a partnership opportunity. The site, which strives to offer the "Earth's biggest selection," offered him the chance to become a preferred merchant and sell his products in the gourmet, sporting goods, and apparel categories. Reeder had some experience selling used books and such in the open-to-all Amazon Marketplace, but he was initially hesitant to become a Pro Merchant because doing so meant he had to buy insurance, raise his prices, speed up the shipping process, and overall begin behaving more like a real business. But the move turned out to be one of the best things Reeder did for his enterprise.

To make selling on Amazon worthwhile, Reeder had to raise his prices across the board to cover the 15 percent to 20 percent fee the site takes for each sale. Amazon won't allow its merchant sellers to price items lower on their own web sites, so Reeder had to begin charging more at www.captaindaves.com, as well. In addition, Amazon sets specific shipping parameters for merchants; with few exceptions, all items must be shipped within two days. "That forced us to change how we do business," Reeder says. "Being an Amazon seller made us grow up to compete with the bigger boys. It used to be, you'd buy something from us, and you'd get it in a week or two."

Though Amazon forced Captain Dave's to grow up, Reeder likes the marketplace because it opened up a different customer base whose buying patterns aren't linked to disaster scares. "Amazon is really great for helping us find those customers who would look for cargo pants but not bugout kits and emergency and survival gear," Reeder says. He now runs his online venture full-time and operates out of a 3,000-square-foot warehouse, not his basement. "Apparel has contributed to our growth a great deal. Boots and pants are some of our staple items. We probably would still be in my basement if we weren't selling those items. It gives us an entrée to a different customer base."

Having a storefront on Amazon also led Captain Dave's to begin selling in yet another online marketplace—eBay. Reeder funnels any customer returns through the auction site. It's a particularly effective channel for getting rid of odd sizes of clothing, say size 4XL paramedic's pants. He has also branched out into offering new merchandise on eBay and is now the site's largest seller of combat boots.

Reeder's business really benefits from its Amazon presence in the fourth quarter when online shopping surges because of the holidays. His sales on Amazon alone routinely triple or quadruple during that period. (By contrast, he might see an uptick of 100 percent on his own web site.) Because of Amazon's strong fourth-quarter performance, Reeder makes sure to supplement his inventory at that time. Sales improve in all online channels around the holidays, Reeder says, but nowhere as much as at Amazon. He believes the site's strong reputation and customer-centric approach are the reasons. "I look at buying a product on Amazon like it used to be buying your computers on IBM," he says. "It's the safe choice."

Amazon protects buyers by processing all payments and then distributing those funds every two weeks to Marketplace and Pro Merchant sellers. That setup also happens to be beneficial for sellers, who have to worry less about fraud and losing money through credit card chargebacks on the site. If Amazon approves a transaction that later turns out to be fraudulent, Reeder still gets paid. Amazon eats the cost of the charge-back. On his own web site and other marketplaces, like eBay, Reeder would be responsible.

Sellers also bear a responsibility in preventing fraud. About 10 percent of the Captain Dave's site sales are to international customers. In channels other than Amazon, Reeder requires payment via PayPal because there's less chance of fraud with an electronic money transfer and because his bank charges more to process international orders. When a customer orders certain high-ticket items—a bullet-resistant vest, for example—Reeder always calls the customer before shipping to make sure the purchase is legitimate. If anything strikes him as fishy about an order, he'll wait and perform additional checks before releasing the order in his warehouse.

"Every now and then someone defrauds us," but not often, he says.

With three channels to choose from, Reeder is very deliberate in deciding which products to sell where. He usually begins by listing items on the Captain Dave's web site, where his selling costs are lower. Amazon carries less financial risk than eBay because there are no listing fees. EBay is, by far, the most expensive and most time-consuming channel with the lowest margins. Add to that the fact that Reeder must pay ChannelAdvisor, his auction management solutions provider, 2 percent for every item he sells there and it becomes clear why Reeder uses eBay only for liquidation and for lower-cost, higher-margin items that he can sell through his eBay store or at a fixed price. Reeder won't list things like a year's supply of Ready Reserve food, which retails for $2,700, on eBay because he'd have to pay $5 to $6 in listing fees alone. "I can list it on Amazon, and I don't pay a dime until I sell it," he notes. Reeder makes two exceptions to this rule. When eBay offers free or discounted listing days, he takes advantage of the discount and posts higher-priced items for sale there. And if there's some newsworthy natural disaster or scare, like Hurricane Katrina or the bird flu, Reeder will pay the fees necessary to initiate auctions for those higher-cost items that are sure to be in demand. "At some point, the next time the bird flu comes into the news, I can put them on eBay and they'll sell like crazy," says Reeder, who's quick to stress that he doesn't hope for such horrible things to happen. "Our business tends to uptick whenever there's a disaster. We did great after Hurricane Katrina because people said, 'This can happen to us.' I would much rather that people are prepared before the disaster strikes than buy from us afterwards."

Though most big sellers find it advantageous to use software like ChannelAdvisor to manage their inventory across multiple channels, Reeder prefers not to use it for his Amazon sales. Instead, he manually uploads inventory to Amazon on a regular basis, converting his inventory database to a flat file that Amazon can recognize. He could easily do the job with the software but doesn't in order to avoid the per-transaction fee that ChannelAdvisor charges. "I was selling on Amazon before getting ChannelAdvisor, and I didn't necessarily want to give them 2 percent on every product I sell through Amazon," he explains. However, Reeder does use technology to its full advantage when it comes to shipping.

Not long after he began selling in the three channels, Reeder noticed that shipping was becoming unmanageable, even though at the time he was handling only about 30 packages a day. He invested in Stone Edge Technologies' Order Manager, a scalable back-office system for multichannel merchants. The program aggregates order data from eBay, Amazon, and the Captain Dave's web site into one database and allows Reeder to batch process shipments and print labels, as well as send out automated e-mails to customers and handle other customer-service tasks, like e-mail, from a single platform. Before signing up with Stone Edge in August 2005, Reeder had to log into his account at each marketplace and process transactions separately, a much more time-consuming endeavor. "It has allowed us to quickly expand and be able to handle more sales," he says.

Though Amazon and eBay each bring in a fair amount of business to Captain Dave's every year, Reeder does everything in his power to drive customers to his web site. That's because the average order amount is higher and his selling costs are lower.

The Captain Dave's web site, which is also mirrored at www .survival-center.com, ranks high in natural search results because it has been on the Internet for years. Both sites are rich with content, specifically free information aimed at helping people survive natural and man-made disasters. "That is still an important objective of ours to have information out there such as when to evacuate, how to evacuate, and how to prepare ahead of time," Reeder says. "That generates traffic, and one day they may come back and buy from us."

Reeder also uses more traditional marketing techniques to promote web site traffic and sales. An electronic newsletter that Reeder says "doesn't go out as often as it should" entices customers to www.captaindaves.com with discounts available only on web site purchases. In addition, eBay and Amazon customers get coupons they can use to purchase again from the Captain Dave's site.

Auctions and Shopping on Yahoo!

3

The Lowdown

Yahoo! is the most popular site on the Web. It is visited daily by nearly one-third of all Internet users who are seeking news and information. Often described as a search engine, Yahoo! is much more than that. It's also an e-commerce marketplace, an auction site, a shopping-comparison engine, and a portal to thousands of merchant stores. It is a fierce competitor to eBay, Amazon, Overstock, and every other e-commerce marketplace. In short, if you're doing business online, Yahoo! is not a channel to be ignored.

You'll learn more in future chapters about how to market your products on the Yahoo! search engine and the Yahoo! Shopping comparison engine. This chapter focuses on how you can use Yahoo! tools to build a fully functional e-commerce site and shows ways to use the company's free auction platform to the best advantage for your business.

Yahoo! hosts more than 40,000 e-commerce stores for merchants of all sizes, from those just tinkering online to big companies whose online sales top $10 million annually. Some pretty big names operate Yahoo! stores: Ben & Jerry's, Callaway Golf, Crabtree & Evelyn, PepsiCo, Sharper Image, and Vermont Teddy Bear, just to name a few.

In total, merchants complete more than $3 billion in transactions annually through their Yahoo!-branded stores and web sites. True, that figure is just a small percentage of the sales generated annually through eBay, but it's large enough to make Yahoo! one of eBay's biggest competitors. Yahoo! offers online entrepreneurs what eBay can't—the tools and infrastructure necessary to build their own branded web sites. You certainly could build an e-commerce site. In fact, you'll read tips for doing so in the next chapter. But if you're not up to the chore technically or financially, or if you don't want to spend the time it takes to build a professional-looking e-tail site, Yahoo! provides a nice shortcut.

Because of Yahoo!'s own reputation as the place to go on the Web when you're looking for something—be it a new pair of shoes or information for a term paper—the search engine delivers a lot of traffic to these stores. Yahoo! stores and their product listings are automatically indexed in all the major search engines, giving the company's merchants a jump start when it comes to driving traffic through search-engine marketing and optimization.

"We really provide a turnkey solution," says Jimmy Duvall, director of e-commerce solutions at Yahoo! "The small business owner can focus primarily on their business. It really removes that huge component of having to build a web site by yourself."

If you decide to use the Yahoo! infrastructure to build an online store rather than doing it from scratch or hiring the job out, you'll be able to choose from three different options, designed and priced to fit businesses of different sizes. Depending on the option you select, you can post as many as 50,000 items for sale in your Yahoo! store with no listing fees. In addition to an online storefront, you'll get Web hosting, inventory management software, marketing tools, and order processing abilities. Prices range from $39.95 a month plus a

1.5 percent fee on every transaction for the starter solution to $299.95 plus a 0.75 percent fee on every transaction for the professional-level solution. You'll read more later in this chapter about what you get at each price point.

In addition to offering Web stores, Yahoo! also operates an online auction site at www.auctions.yahoo.com. Unlike other auction marketplaces, Yahoo!'s is completely free. There are no listing costs, final-value fees, or other expenses associated with doing business on the site. On any given day, there are between 800,000 and 900,000 active auctions on the site. In a month's time, about 60,000 of those items end up selling. The sell-through rate for Yahoo! Auctions is only about 0.2 percent, which makes it one of the least attractive auction sites for sellers. You may find that you have to relist an item multiple times in order to sell it, and even then the auction may attract only a single bidder. Despite these limitations, Yahoo! Auctions may still fit into your multichannel online marketing strategy because it's totally free. It's a good place to park "dead" stock, and you may also experience some success if you focus on niche categories and aggressively market to your existing customer base.

Getting Started

Yahoo! makes it fairly easy to turn your idea for an e-commerce site into a reality for a relatively small initial investment. Using the tools provided, you can build and stock the store yourself, even if you don't have any computer programming or HTML skills. This is more of a cookie-cutter approach, best suited for smaller sellers who don't mind using stock templates in their web site design. If you prefer a more customized design, Yahoo! also allows you to create a store using pages that you've designed with Web publishing tools like Front Page, Dreamweaver, or the free Yahoo! SiteBuilder application. You also have the option of hiring someone to create the look and feel of the design while still taking advantage of the Yahoo! infrastructure.

Your first step to becoming an e-tailer is choosing the Web package that suits your business in terms of both cost and functionality. Each package includes some standard services, including a personalized domain name (or Web address) for your store, a secure shopping cart, 20 gigabytes of file storage space, 500 gigabytes of bandwidth monthly, a shipping rate calculator, and inventory management tools. The more money you spend, the more features and functionality you get.

Yahoo!'s entry-level store product is called Merchant Starter and costs $39.95 a month plus a one-time $50 setup fee. In addition, you'll pay a 1.5 percent commission to Yahoo! for every sale made through your online store. This package is targeted to smaller merchants who expect sales of less than $12,000 a month or $144,000 annually. Among its limitations, you won't be able to integrate real-time order data with your back-end inventory systems, nor will you be able to batch process shipments directly from your computer by exporting them to UPS Worldship. With the Starter package, you can't process coupons or gift certificates or cross-sell items to your customers at checkout and other times during the shopping process. Finally, you won't be able to track customer movements on your web site by monitoring which pages they visit or analyzing their searches to see how they find products.

Yahoo!'s two other store packages allow you to do all these things. The midpriced option is called Merchant Standard and costs $99.95 per month, plus a 1 percent per-transaction fee. The setup cost is $50. This solution is meant for medium-sized e-tailers, those who expect monthly revenues of $12,000 to $80,000. The final option is Merchant Professional, which costs $50 to set up and $299.95 per month. Commissions are lower—just 0.75 percent of every transaction—and the product is targeted to larger, high-volume merchants who expect to sell at least $80,000 in merchandise every month. It's the most scalable solution, and it's the best fit for companies with a huge inventory.

Next, you'll need to come up with a name for your Web store and register the domain. You can do this yourself at one of the domain registration sites like Network Solutions, Whois, and GoDaddy.com, or directly through Yahoo! It's probably a good idea to register the name for several years or set up the automatic renewal feature so you don't lose your Web address down the road.

Once you've completed these two steps, it's time to begin building your site, either by using the tools that Yahoo! provides, by designing HTML pages, or by hiring out the design to a professional. For specific instructions on how to do this, download Yahoo!'s 380-page "Getting Started Guide" at http://smallbusiness.yahoo.com/merchant/gstartdwnload.php. During this step, you'll plan the navigation and determine exactly what your site will look like. At this stage, Yahoo! recommends creating an outline—something most Web developers do to organize a site's content. According to Yahoo!, these are some of the elements and navigational components you'll want to include in that outline:

- An attractive and informative home page where you'll promote your most popular products, publicize special offers, and advertise new items. The home page should include links to section pages, where your customers will find different categories of products.

- Section pages that provide customers with an overview of the different categories of products you sell.

- Item pages that include photographs, descriptions, and pricing information about every product in your inventory.

- A help page where customers can find out more information about your company and how to contact you with questions about products and orders. This is also a good place to provide information about your return policy, shipping, and taxes.

- A privacy page that informs customers how you will protect their personal and financial data and your policies for sharing that information with third parties.

- Shopping cart and checkout pages.
- Navigation links that appear in the same order on every page of the web site.

In addition to these recommended components, you can include any others that you feel with enhance your customers' shopping experiences and improve the functionality of your site. Some merchants, for example, have a blog on their e-commerce site where they include news and reviews of new products. Others include buying guides, glossaries, and other educational information. You might choose to post press releases or articles about your business. Brad and Jennifer Fallon of My Wedding Favors have a Message Boards link in their Yahoo! store where brides can chat about products, ask questions of one another, and share wedding-planning tips and stories.

Once you've built the walls of your virtual store, so to speak, you'll need to start stocking the shelves by uploading products into inventory. Yahoo! provides sellers with a tool called Catalog Manager, which is essentially a database where you can enter various product attributes, including item name, item number, description, price, size, and quantity available. (You're able to define the various fields and add customized ones, as well.) In addition, you can include a photograph of every item in your inventory at this stage. You can manually enter all of your store items into Catalog Manager or upload a file containing that data from your existing inventory system. The upload file must be in .csv (short for comma-separated values) format.

At this point, your site is almost ready to go live. But first, you must make some important decisions that will apply to every transaction you conduct. Within the Yahoo! software, you'll need to answer some questions and run a series of Wizards to set up your shipping, taxation, payment, and order processing preferences.

By this stage, you should determine what types of payments you will accept from customers. You can opt to accept only PayPal payments, but doing so may drive some customers away. When you open an online store, you should probably set up a merchant account with a bank so you'll be able to process credit card and debit card payments online. You can apply for a merchant account with Yahoo!'s partner, Paymentech, or with any other credit-card processing company that is compatible with the First Data Services Nashville platform.

Once all these steps are completed, your Yahoo! store is ready to open for business. Your next job—and probably the hardest one—is attracting customers and exceeding their expectations with the products and customer service you offer.

I also promised to tell you how to sell in the Yahoo! Auctions marketplace. You'll be pleased to learn that establishing an account and posting items for auction is much simpler than building a fully functional Yahoo! Web site. From the Yahoo! Auctions home page (www.auctions.yahoo.com), you'll need to register as a user. (If you already have a Yahoo! E-mail address or user ID for forums and message boards, you can sign up using that information. Before you're able to sell, Yahoo! verifies your user information by asking for your name, address, telephone number, and driver's license or Social Security number. This is the site's attempt to block fraudulent buyers and sellers.

Now you're ready to begin listing items for auction. You can do so manually, following the step-by-step instructions online. You may also use any compatible auction management software or Yahoo! Sellers Manager or Bulk Loader.

The process for listing items for sale at Yahoo! Auctions is nearly identical to posting products on eBay. You'll choose a category to list your item in, then create the actual auction ad by writing a headline and description. Yahoo! gives you the option of including 10 photos, three of which can be uploaded directly to the Auctions site. Your auction can run anywhere from two days to 10 days and you can set the exact starting date and time and closing time so that the auction ends when traffic is at its maximum.

As on eBay, you set the opening bid price (remember that traffic on Yahoo! Auctions is lower, so it's probably unwise to start bidding at

99 cents unless you don't mind selling the item at that price), and you also have the option of setting a "Buy Now" price.

During the listing process, you can choose to block bidders with feedback ratings lower than a particular threshold if you're fearful of fraud. Yahoo! Auctions offers sellers a few other unique options to make selling on the site easier and less time-consuming. If your auction receives any last-minute bids, you can opt to have it extended by five minutes. And if the item doesn't sell, you can instruct Yahoo! to automatically resubmit it as many as five times.

Yahoo! Auctions sellers get to define their own payment terms. On the site, you'll be able to accept PayPal, credit-card, and escrow payments, if you choose, as well as personal checks, money orders, and cashier's checks.

How It Works

Yahoo! Auctions is a straight auction site where bidders compete with one another for merchandise. The person who's willing to pay the most wins the auction. Sellers do have the option of selling products at fixed prices—a more traditional e-commerce approach—but competitive auctions dominate. Therefore, there's really no need for a lengthy discussion here of how auction selling works because the previous chapter about eBay tells all you need to know about that.

I will, however, reiterate here a few points about the binding nature of auctions and the importance of customer service. Once an auction closes, buyers and sellers enter into a binding contract. Buyers are obligated to pay promptly for the item (and any associated costs, like shipping). Upon receiving that payment, the seller is required to ship the item right away, in the condition promised. Should a buyer fail to hold up his or her end of the bargain, you should post negative feedback and report that behavior to Yahoo!, so site managers can take steps to rectify the problem or block the person from bidding on additional auctions. Expect the same thing to happen to you if you fail to fulfill your duties as a seller. After a transaction is completed, it's important to leave feedback—whether it's positive or negative—for the other party. This will help fellow users determine if they want to do business with that person in the future. When you leave positive feedback for others, they're more likely to reciprocate.

Now on to our discussion about the ins and outs of operating a Yahoo! e-commerce store. This is your very own web site, and as such, you get to make all the rules about how it operates. You're in control of the appearance of your online store, and yet set the policies about what and how you sell. Pricing is purely within your hands, and you alone decide what forms of payments you'll accept, how and when you'll ship products to customers, and whether you'll accept returns or offer refunds. More so than in the other channels, you have the ability to build a brand, cultivate repeat customers, and reward them for their loyalty.

"Very rarely will a buyer in a traditional marketplace come back and find the same seller and buy from them again," Yahoo's Jimmy Duvall says. "That buyer is really motivated by price alone. How most businesses become successful with a Yahoo! store is by establishing themselves in a particular segment and marketing themselves to that segment."

Having your own e-commerce store certainly provides you with a lot more freedom. But with that freedom come additional responsibilities and some extra marketing challenges that you don't encounter in the structured online marketplaces.

The hardest reality of hanging up your own shingle is that you alone will be responsible for driving traffic to your site, much as you would if you opened a bricks-and-mortar store. Yahoo, like any popular shopping center, will bring customers to your threshold, but you have to convince them to walk through your door by stocking popular products and effectively marketing and advertising them. These are just a few other ways you'll win and keep customers: competitive pricing, stellar customer service, a changing merchandise assortment, attractive discounts and offers, and a reputable standing.

Because your store site will be part of Yahoo!'s Shopping portal, it will have increased visibility compared with other e-tailers. However, according to Yahoo!, few shoppers actually drill down through the Shopping portal's categories to find a particular product. Instead, they're much more likely to enter product-specific search terms on the Yahoo! main page or on the Shopping home page. For that reason, you'll need to make sure that you use enough—and the right—keywords in your product descriptions so that your items are indexed correctly and show up at the top of search results. Otherwise, you'll have difficulty driving traffic to your Web store and your sales will suffer. If you're not already doing so to promote your online auctions and products for sale on other sites, now is the time to consider search-engine optimization, paid online advertising, and listing your products in the comparison-shopping engines. (Read Chapter 6 for advice on how to do this as well as the proven strategies being employed by other online merchants.)

When opening a Yahoo! store, don't neglect your existing customers in your marketing efforts. If you're smart, you've been collecting their names, e-mail addresses, and perhaps their merchandise preferences in a customer database. If you haven't been diligent about this, you may be able to go back through your "sold" records on eBay, Amazon, and elsewhere and reconstruct your selling history. If you have a PayPal account, you can do the same thing in the account history pages. Send your customers an e-mail letting them know that you've opened a Yahoo! store. Give them an incentive to visit the store by offering a special discount or coupon. Many Web merchants send out regular e-mail newsletters to customers who choose to receive them, in which they advertise new products and offer special promotions. This is a great way to keep traffic flowing to your site, but please make sure that you have your customers' permission to market to them. Another great way to drive traffic to your site is by having a weblog, or blog, that is updated regularly. The owner of one Yahoo! scrapbooking store offers product reviews and how-to project guides on her blog. Brad and Jennifer Fallon's blog for My Wedding Favors includes wedding-planning tips as well as articles of interest to brides-to-be and grooms-to-be.

Even if you're able to draw visitors to your e-commerce store, you may notice that this traffic isn't converting to sales. Some of that may be attributed to pricing and the products you have available. But questions about your site's legitimacy or security may be the cause as well. Despite all the worries about fraud on eBay and other web sites, for the most part consumers view these marketplaces as safe. They feel safe buying from merchants on these platforms because they believe that the sites will protect them and provide a refund should anything go wrong with the transaction. Unfortunately, the same level of confidence doesn't extend to individual e-commerce sites, unless they happen to be associated with a well-known brand, like Pepsi, Best Buy, or the National Basketball Association (NBA). However, there are things you can do to ease these worries and break down the barriers that may be keeping customers from buying from you.

First, if you have a great reputation in another marketplace, publicize that on your e-commerce site. Link to your feedback ratings on eBay, Amazon, and Overstock so potential customers can view your history of good customer service. Also, take advantage of Yahoo! Shopping's rating system, which allows customers to rate your service, once immediately after checkout and again about two weeks later after they've received their merchandise.

In addition, sign up for some of the third-party verification and rating services, such as VeriSign, buySAFE, and BizRate. Displaying these credentials on your Web store will engender great consumer confidence and increase the likelihood that visitors to your Web store will buy from you.

What Sells Best

The Internet is a microcosm of the world, and on the Web you'll find everything for sale that you'd find in the real world. That means you're free to sell just about anything in your e-commerce store. Of course, you'll reap more success with some products than others.

A good rule of thumb when opening a Yahoo! store is to focus on new items, unless you're in a business like antiques, vintage clothing, or restoration car parts, where customers aren't looking for new products. Customers searching for used items will turn to auction sites and other online marketplaces to find them before searching the broader Web. So, if you open a store that sells used goods, you're never going to be the first place customers think of to look for the product. But for new items, customers are just as likely to visit a search site or a comparison-shopping engine as they are to browse over to eBay or Amazon. If you promote your store and your products correctly, you should be able to capture a large amount of this search business.

It's difficult to pinpoint particular categories of products that sell well in Web stores. Success ultimately depends on the site, pricing, branding, and marketing. But you'd be hard-pressed to fail if you focus on high-demand items, such as computers, digital cameras, MP3 players, and other consumer electronics, and offer competitive prices, prompt delivery, and good customer service. Niche categories can also be very profitable, and these would include things shoppers can't find in abundance in their local stores. One Yahoo! merchant, for example, operates a successful pet store targeted specifically at owners of ferrets. Most hometown pet stores (even the big chains like Petco and Petsmart) wouldn't even have an aisle devoted to these animals This Yahoo! e-tailer offers a full-breadth of products for ferrets and their owners and does quite well for himself. (I'm sure that if he'd opened a bricks-and-mortar store specializing in these types of products he would have gone out of business in a year because there wouldn't have been enough local demand to keep the store open. On the Web, however, his business is thriving.)

Some niches aren't nearly as unusual. Another successful Yahoo! store sells baby furniture and other items for the nursery. This particular merchant chose to build a Web store after first trying to market the products on eBay. Because of eBay's fee structure and competition from other merchants, she found it impossible to turn a profit *and* offer the level of customer service she wanted to.

Brad Fallon, who was a search-engine optimization expert before opening his own e-commerce site, recommends that merchants figure out if there's an online market for their products before going to the trouble and expense of building a Web store. "A lot of people try to sell products online that people just aren't searching for," he says. If you're already selling in another online marketplace, you may have a good idea of the demand level for your products. If you don't, there's a quick way to find out. Browse on over to Overture (now a division of Yahoo! Search Marketing) and use the Keyword Selector Tool to analyze the search volume for the products you're hoping to sell online. It will provide you with statistics on the number of people who are searching within your product niche and it will also recommend additional search terms that you can use in your marketing and keyword advertising.

If you're planning to open an account with Yahoo! Auctions, you'll need to be even more careful about what you sell because of the low traffic and conversion rates. Niche collectibles sell better than any other types of products on Yahoo! Auctions. Look to this marketplace if your business is coins, paper money, and stamps; sports cards and memorabilia; books and comics; toys, games, and hobbies; and other collectibles. Other popular categories include jewelry and watches (about 6,000 such items sell every month on Yahoo! Auctions) and clothing and accessories (with about 5,000 items selling every month). Music, electronics, and cameras are other strong categories, each closing about 2,200 sales every month.

Pros and Cons

Opening your own e-commerce store is an excellent way to expand your business and build your brand. It's also probably the best way to cultivate repeat business, which will save you money and contribute to profitability in the long run. As any business professor will tell you, it's much less expensive to keep an existing customer than it is to acquire a new one.

"EBay is a good feeder into e-commerce," says Yahoo!'s Duvall. "It doesn't necessarily allow a small business to create a unique presence of their own that's branded and really build a unique brand. EBay is the great equalizer, unfortunately, where you can't differentiate."

Yahoo! Merchant Solutions provides its customers with a fairly inexpensive and uncomplicated way to become e-commerce web site operators. If you were to build a Web store from scratch, you'd likely encounter more roadblocks and wind up spending more money, though your site would be tailor-made just for your business.

With your own Yahoo! Web store, you're free from many of the financial constraints that you'll encounter in other marketplaces. You can list as many items for sale as you want, without incurring per-item listing fees. Unfortunately, Yahoo! isn't fee-free. Keep in mind that you will be responsible for Yahoo!'s monthly subscription charge for Web hosting, and you'll also pay a per-transaction commission. In addition, you'll owe money on the back end to your merchant account bank if you choose to accept credit cards. Most credit card processing companies charge a monthly fee for service, and they also levy a flat fee for every transaction and take a percentage from every sale.

Beware of the other associated fees that come with running your own web site. As a Yahoo! merchant, you're eligible for some discounts on search-engine advertising and listings in comparison-shopping engines, but these necessary marketing fees can quickly add up. You could easily spend hundreds of dollars every month—and more as your business grows—on online advertising, search-engine optimization, ad performance tracking, and e-mail marketing.

The Yahoo! Auctions site provides you with yet another channel for marketing your goods. Its biggest advantage is that it's free and therefore risk-free. You can list items for sale without worrying about draining your cash flow or eroding your profit margins. However, the auction site is not the most robust marketplace, increasing the likelihood that you'll have to relist items multiple times before selling them. This won't cost money in terms of listing fees, but you won't be able to turn your inventory as quickly, and that is an expense you should be mindful of. For that reason, you might choose to use Yahoo! Auctions as a liquidation outlet. (If you use this strategy, price aggressively. At this point, your goal should be to make room in your warehouse for more profitable items. You want to get rid of slow sellers quickly and inexpensively, and the best way to do this is through discounting.)

For some reason, Yahoo! auctioneers seem to have to deal with more fraud than their counterparts on other sites. Perhaps that's because anyone who has an email address can bid on a Yahoo! Auctions without first signing up as a registered user. To avoid being victimized, you may want to consider banning people with low or no feedback from bidding on your auctions. Another precaution you can take is to wait a few days after receiving payment before shipping the product. This applies even when the person pays with a credit card or PayPal. If the purchase is determined to be suspect, PayPal and the credit card companies can reverse the charges and you as the merchant may have little recourse for recovering your money.

It's important not to let these challenges keep you from exploring other channels, like opening a Yahoo! store or participating on the Yahoo! Auctions platform. But as always, you should be informed of the pros and the cons so you can choose the best, most profitable multichannel approach for your online business.

Action Plan

Here are the steps for getting your business up and running on Yahoo!:

- ✔ Determine whether there is a broad online market for your products by checking to see how many Web users are searching for the products that you plan to sell. You can use tools at Yahoo! Search Marketing to determine this information.

✔ From the Yahoo! Shopping page, visit a variety of Yahoo! Web stores of various sizes to see if the format works for your business.

✔ Figure out the financial outlook of your business. How much merchandise do you realistically expect to sell through your own Web store in the first year? The fifth year? The tenth year?

✔ Choose a Yahoo! Merchant Solutions package that fits your current revenue expectations, as well as your projections, so you're not faced with the prospect of having to rebuild your e-commerce site as your business grows.

✔ Draft the outline for your Web store. What will it look like? How many products will you list for sale? In how many categories? How will customers navigate your site? What will be featured on your home page? What additional features will you include on the web site?

✔ Decide whether you will accept credit card payments or PayPal. If so, sign up for a business-level PayPal account and merchant account with a bank so you'll be able to process payments the day your site goes live.

✔ Create your inventory catalog, including specific information that customers and search engines will use to find your products.

✔ Consider having a soft opening for your web site, so you can make any changes or work out any glitches before becoming overwhelmed with orders.

✔ Inform your existing customers that you have opened a Yahoo! store. Offer them a discount on their first purchase or provide some other incentive, such as a free gift, to drive traffic to your web site.

✔ Promote your business beyond your existing customer base through online keyword advertising, search-engine marketing, and comparison-shopping engines.

Yahoo! Success Story

My Wedding Favors

Brad and Jennifer Fallon got more than they bargained for when they walked down the aisle in 2003. Their nuptials spawned a multimillion-dollar e-commerce site that four years later has morphed into a veritable Internet empire consisting of more than a half-dozen sites. But that's what happens when a bride who is determined to find something different for her wedding marries a groom who is an expert in search-engine optimization.

When Jennifer was planning her wedding, she turned to the Internet to find favors for her guests. Specifically, she was looking for place card holders for the reception tables. Finding examples online wasn't the problem. In fact, Jennifer was overwhelmed by just how many different merchants online were selling wedding favors. But she was underwhelmed by the quality and variety.

Such a disappointing search may have left some brides-to-be frustrated and frantic to find the perfect place card holders somewhere else. But Jennifer was no bridezilla. Her fruitless Internet shopping experience didn't ruin her wedding; rather, it gave her and her fiancé, Brad, a great idea for a business. They decided to start their own online wedding favors site and to distinguish theirs from the competition with broader merchandise offerings, better design, and more targeted online marketing.

Through their web site, MyWeddingFavors.com, the Fallons carry about 600 different wedding favors, as well as bridesmaids' gifts, groomsmen's gifts, and other wedding accessories. They ship about 800 orders a day from their warehouse in Norcross, Georgia, near Atlanta. In addition, the Fallons operate several other e-commerce sites, such as elegantweddingbands.com and qualitybridalshoes.com, that they cross promote to couples planning to marry. The Fallons are also behind several other nonrelated Web stores, including cornerstork-babygifts.com, electric-scooters-galore.com, luckycigars.com, and in-stantpokerchips.com.

Just a few months after getting hitched, Brad and Jennifer launched MyWeddingFavors.com with an initial investment of less than $1,000, including $50 spent on a Yahoo! store. They chose Yahoo! specifically because it was a quick, easy, and affordable way to build a Web store. And although the business has grown tremendously in just three years, the Fallons are still proud Yahoo! merchants, since that solution easily scaled with their business.

With the rest of their initial $1,000 investment, the Fallons bought merchandise at the Atlanta Gift Mart and funded an online advertising and search-engine optimization campaign. Their Yahoo! store launched with just 40 products, but within the first month sales reached $11,000. By the third month—on the strength of Web advertising and marketing—monthly sales rose to $80,000. Within six months, the Fallons' sales totaled $150,000 a month, or $1.8 million on an annualized basis. Now just three years into their venture, the Fallons are at the helm of a $15 million company, with one-third of revenues coming from their wedding favors site. They've both left full-time jobs to run their entrepreneurial venture.

Those statistics are impressive for any fledgling Web venture, but even more so when you consider the nature of the wedding favors business. The Fallons have very little repeat business because their customers are buying for a single special event. Luckily, however, they can count on bulk buyers. Depending on the size of their celebration, couples may buy dozens, if not hundreds, of the same item from MyWeddingFavors.com, be it bottle stoppers, candles, or chocolates.

But the true reason for the Fallons' success is that they drive a huge volume of traffic to their Yahoo! store and convert a significant percentage of that traffic into sales. The Fallons went into business knowing that there is a huge demand for wedding favors, decor, and related items. That is yet another key factor behind their success. Using data easily available from search engines and other Web search ranking services, Brad Fallon determined that 150,000 people every month were doing Internet searches for the term *wedding favors*. Brad did additional research at Overture (now a division of Yahoo! Search Marketing) to determine the other types of wedding-related items Internet users were searching for. He used that data as the basis for the company's first online keyword advertising campaign, recognizing that each search represents a potential customer.

"I used to teach search-engine marketing and so we came out of the gate with a very specific plan to have our web site rank in the search engines," Brad says. He initially accomplished that through paid search, although now MyWeddingFavors.com ranks high in natural search results, as well.

"We started with some nice products and got traffic immediately," he says. "We spent money on Yahoo! to get people to see our site when they were searching for the stuff we sell."

Buying traffic is important, insists Brad, whether you're a new or an established online retailer. "Some people put up a web site and cross their fingers. They don't buy traffic," he observes. Even now, although MyWeddingFavors.com ranks at the top of the natural search results whenever someone searches for the term "wedding favors" on Yahoo! or Google, Fallon still spends about $80,000 a month on keyword advertising campaigns with Yahoo!, Google, and other popular search engines.

In addition to paying for high search placement, Brad optimizes his web sites so that they rank high in natural search results. Each product page is designed so that it can easily be crawled by spiders, programs that automatically fetch web pages and feed them to the search engines. For example, he liberally uses keywords within item titles and descriptions to increase the likelihood that his sites will show up when Web browsers search for specific terms. In addition, Fallon uses web site meta tags to his full advantage. Meta tags are special HTML coding included within a web site that provide information about what the page is about. Meta tags aren't actually displayed as text on a web page, but they offer key details to the search engines and can improve a site's ranking in search results. Finally, Brad trades links with other sites—he links to them and they link to him. Doing this also improves his rankings within the search engines.

If you visit MyWeddingFavors.com, you'll notice that the product categories themselves are quite descriptive: Unique Wedding Favors, Bridal Shower Favors, Place Card Holders, Silver Wedding Favors, Candle Wedding Favors, Wine Wedding Favors, Golf Wedding Favors, Spring Wedding Favors, Practical Wedding Favors, Personalized Favors, Chocolate Wedding Favors, and Edible Wedding Favors, for example. The category names include specific terms that customers are likely to search for at Yahoo!, Google, or MSN. If you type any of these terms into one of the search engines, a listing for MyWeddingFavors.com is likely to show up as one of the top results. If you click through on the link, you'll be directed to a landing page featuring items in that specific category.

"We promote all the products that we have," Brad says. "Most people that originally come to the web site aren't looking for a particular product. They're typing in 'unique wedding favors,' 'cheap wedding favors,' and usually those terms will come up in the free search results."

Brad certainly knows what he's talking about when it comes to search-engine optimization. He's a self-described computer geek, not the kind of person who comes to mind when you think of the dictionary definition of *cool*. But Brad has positioned himself as the "coolest guy on the planet," according to Google search results, by using these same search-engine marketing and optimization techniques. Go ahead, search for the term. You'll find a link to www.bradfallon.com, his search-engine optimization consulting business. (Apparently, there's a battle raging among search marketing gurus for the title. At press time for this book, Brad still held the top spot.)

As Brad will tell you, it isn't enough to simply drive traffic to your e-commerce store. You also have to do things to convert those browsers into paying customers. That job begins on the home page; you want to hook customers immediately with attractive products so that they delve deeper into your site, rather than hitting the back button to return to the indexed search rankings.

On its home page, MyWeddingFavors.com features images, pricing, and descriptions of 15 of the company's most unique wedding favors. There are navigational links leading to every category of product the company sells, but seven popular and seasonal categories are featured at the top of the page, just below the banner logo. In addition, the Fallons boast of their five-star Yahoo! Shopping rating and their low-price guarantee on the first screen of their home page. Without having to scroll down the home page, users see a toll-free customer service telephone number for MyWeddingFavors.com, and they can also click for live online help from a wedding consultant.

Essentially, MyWeddingFavors.com answers on its home page almost any question a new customer would have. There's a quick welcome note from Jennifer in which she invites customer feedback and tells shoppers how to ask for help if they encounter any difficulty on the site. There are links to the site's best sellers and to MyWedding Favors.TV, where brides can watch a video about trends in wedding favors. Logos from Visa, MasterCard, American Express, Discover, and UPS indicate what payment and shipping methods the site uses. Shoppers can click to see comments from previous customers, and they learn that the site has been judged safe and secure by the Better Business Bureau Online, Reliability Program, HackerSafe, and TRUSTe.

"You need to get customers involved in your site and get them to click on something off your home page and into other areas of the site," Brad says, noting that just by changing a few things about his home page he has been able to increase conversion rates significantly in the past year. "When it comes to e-commerce, there are two issues. One is traffic and one is conversion. How do I get more people to my web site and how do I get more web site visitors to take the desired action of buying something?"

In addition to marketing, the Fallons grew their business by listening to what their customers had to say. Jennifer read every e-mail she received from brides. From this feedback she got the idea of including more practical items in pretty packaging in the inventory mix. Unable to find a good source of these types of products, the Fallons partnered with another couple, college friends of Brad's from China, to manufacture the items themselves. They market the private-label products under the Kate Aspen brand name and sell them directly to online customers and wholesale them to other purveyors of wedding favors. The wholesale business now accounts for about one-third of the Fallons' annual revenues.

"There's a big misconception that importing products directly from Asian factories is impossible for the average person," says Brad, who now leads annual trips to China to teach other businesspeople about importing. "But it's not. Anyone can do it with the right information and the right introductions. Yes, there is a language barrier and a fair bit of paperwork, but it's entirely doable. The hardest part is getting started and meeting the right people."

Yahoo! Success Story

Harbor Sweets

In 1973, Benneville Strohecker began making handmade chocolates in the basement of his home in Salem, Massachusetts. The hobby soon morphed into a business, as Strohecker started selling his sweet confections to mail-order customers. Within four years, Strohecker had moved the operation from his home into a tiny candy factory in the seaport town. That same year, a young college student named Phyllis Leblanc landed on the doorstep of Harbor Sweets, looking for a part-time job that would be more appealing and fulfilling than slinging burgers and fries at the local Burger King or McDonald's.

Strohecker hired Leblanc as a part-time candy dipper involved in the production of the company's original signature handmade chocolates, Sweet Sloops. The sailboat-shaped chocolates have an almond butter crunch center that is double dipped in white and dark chocolate and dusted with a coating of crushed pecans Leblanc spent her hours dipping one Sweet Sloop after another into chocolate, while also soaking up some important business lessons.

Leblanc never left Harbor Sweets. In 1981, while still a student, she was given the position of wholesale marketing manager to support the chocolate line's expansion into retail stores. A year later after graduation, Leblanc joined the company full-time. In 1999, with founder Strohecker looking to cut back on his hours, Leblanc completed a leveraged buyout of Harbor Sweets. She's now leading the privately held company in its latest incarnation as a growing Internet retailer.

As it has done since the 1970s, Harbor Sweets still sells its chocolates directly to consumers through a glossy catalog that is mailed out several times a year. In addition, Harbor Sweets chocolate are available at more than 100 gift and gourmet stores nationwide, most of them clustered in the company's home state of Massachusetts and elsewhere in New England. In addition, Harbor Sweets makes custom chocolates for high-profile nonprofits like the Smithsonian Institution, the Guggenheim Museum, the Metropolitan Museum of Art, the Boston Pops, and the Boston Symphony. And then there's the Web store, which has opened up a broader base of consumers and custom orders for the company.

Harbor Sweets actually has been online for a relatively long time—about eight years. But only recently have Internet sales taken off as the company invested more in online advertising and search-engine marketing and experimented with sales in multiple online channels. Mail-order purchases and wholesale accounts still account for the majority of Harbor Sweet's $3 million in annual revenues. But online sales are growing at the fastest pace, about 20 percent annually. And Leblanc definitely anticipates those numbers will increase as Harbor Sweets devotes more resources to promoting its online business. "Our Web sales are about 16 percent of the total business, which is pretty significant in just a couple of years," she says, noting that the Web has helped Harbor Sweets expand its customer base beyond regional markets. "I feel that we get a lot of new business through our web site. A lot of people who do a search for chocolate discover us online. These are customers we would never reach otherwise because we just don't know how to go out and find them. That's the beauty of the Web."

When an employee suggested that Harbor Sweets open a Web store in 1998, the company's executives signed up for Yahoo! Merchant Solutions rather than hiring a developer to build it. "We began with Yahoo! because it was the simplest way to get started," Leblanc explains. Doing so didn't cost a lot of money, and as an added bonus, Harbor Sweets employees didn't need a lot of special expertise to run the web site.

However, given the company's inexperience with Web creation, Harbor Sweets executives opted to outsource that part of the site development to a skilled web site design firm. But they kept administrative and marketing functions in-house—an arrangement that still exists today.

Any business contemplating opening an e-commerce store should consider who will actually do the work of designing and maintaining that site and whether those functions will be outsourced or handled in-house, Leblanc says. For Harbor Sweets, then and now, those decisions are made based on what's most cost-effective for the business.

A few years ago, Harbor Sweets entered into a partnership with one of the Web's biggest retailers and began selling its chocolates in the gourmet food category on Amazon.com. At the time, Leblanc projected that the partnership with Amazon would result in 10 percent annual revenue growth for her company, but that channel didn't pay off quite as she expected. "That was actually pretty disappointing," she says. The company ultimately decided to end the partnership and focus on driving more sales directly to the Harbor Sweets web site.

Though it didn't prove as financially rewarding as Leblanc had hoped, the Amazon partnership was not a complete failure for Harbor Sweets. Indeed, the company learned some important lessons about how to handle search marketing to customers. On the advice of Amazon's experts, Harbor Sweets indexed its products so they'd show up in the results whenever someone searched for any type of chocolate at Amazon. It sounded like a smart strategy, based on the assumption that more exposure would translate into more sales for Harbor Sweets. But this strategy didn't take into account just how fickle chocolate lovers can be. People searching for dark chocolate want to buy dark chocolate. They don't want to see results for milk chocolate or white chocolate. Ditto for people searching for milk chocolate and white chocolate confections. "You get more presence," Leblanc acknowledges, "but it's disappointing for consumers."

That experience has served as an important lesson as Harbor Sweets implements its own search-engine advertising and marketing campaigns. The key to a successful campaign—be it paid or natural search—is to identify those terms that motivated buyers are most likely to use in their Web searches. Leblanc's not sure that there's a surefire strategy that works every time, especially in her industry and for her company in particular. Harbor Sweets products are more than tasty treats; they also reference a particular lifestyle. The company's Classic Nautical line, which includes Sweet Sloops, shell-shaped candies and chocolate wafer embossed with nautical designs, are inspired by the New England seacoast. Another line, Dark Horse Chocolates, features images of horses and riders. And the Hunt Collection is inspired by the traditional foxhunt.

Despite Harbor Sweets' growing popularity, people don't necessarily associate chocolates with equestrian sports, sailing, or foxhunting, Leblanc says, so they're unlikely to search the Web for the terms in combination. Therefore, Harbor Sweets must take a broader approach when marketing its products online, emphasizing such terms as handmade chocolates, gift chocolates, and custom chocolates. Of course, the broader the search term, the more competitive the marketplace and the more difficult it is to be indexed high in the search engine rankings. In the case of Harbor Sweets, the solution is to spend more on search advertising by bidding more for those terms that are most relevant for the company's customers. "We have been exploring some opportunities to do a little bit more marketing through the search engines to move our name up just by allocating more money to it," Leblanc says.

Because there's so much riding on these campaigns, Harbor Sweets monitors its online advertising very closely and tracks the performance of various keywords to determine which campaigns are paying off by delivering the most web site visitors and paying customers. "That's one of the beauties of doing any kind of Web advertising" compared to print or broadcast advertising, Leblanc says. "It's much easier to track your response to any ad. If you're advertising on the Web, you can track how that person came to you a lot more readily. You have a better record of your advertising and whether it's working and can reallocate your resources accordingly."

As Harbor Sweets transitions from a traditional catalog retailer to an e-commerce business, the company is finding both high- and low-tech ways to reach out to existing and potential customers. Even as Web sales have grown, Harbor Sweets continues to mail out glossy catalogs to thousands of shoppers nationwide. The difference now, however, is that the web site features very prominently in the catalog. The company's Web address (www.harborsweets.com) appears on every page, and that's a deliberate attempt to plant the URL in customers' minds so they'll order from Harbor Sweets even if they've thrown the catalog away. The Web address also makes an appearance in any printed materials Harbor Sweets sends out, and it's referenced in all print and broadcast advertisements the company runs. "The beauty of the Web is that people can seek you out whenever they want you," Leblanc says. "The Internet offers a very simple way for people to access your company. They can stumble across you, whereas for us to send someone a catalog at the exact moment that they're interested in buying chocolate is a very difficult thing to do."

Harbor Sweets also maintains a customer database. Those who opt in to receive e-mails from the company often find notices of special offers, discounts, and new products in their in-boxes. E-mail lets Harbor Sweets control its direct marketing budget—it costs virtually nothing to send out an e-mail message to thousands of people—and enables the company to run last-minute sales and promotions, while quickly spreading the word about them.

Transitioning more business to the Web has resulted in some growing pains for Harbor Sweets. Having a web site, even one operated on a reliable platform like Yahoo!, requires constant maintenance and improvements. Employees at Harbor Sweets are tasked with making sure that the site remains current at all times, which can be quite a chore for a company that is constantly promoting seasonal items as well as chocolates from its core product line of 150 different products. But this maintenance is important, both in terms of the company's reputation with customers and its efforts to promote sales by constantly rolling out seasonal treats. For example, Leblanc says, you want Valentine's Day chocolates to be available as soon as customers start thinking about buying them for their sweethearts. But you don't want those heart-shaped boxes appearing on your home page on February 15.

And Web customers have different demands than do people who call or send in a catalog order. When you have a web site, sometimes customers have the perception that you're open 24 hours a day, seven days a week. If you really want to be competitive on the Web, you're going to have to meet that expectation, Leblanc says, noting that Harbor Sweets now staffs its toll-free customer service line around the clock, primarily to respond to questions from Web buyers from around the country. Being on the Web has also changed fulfillment at Harbor Sweets. Online customers have a buy-it-now, get-it-tomorrow mindset. Harbor Sweets doesn't quite meet that standard, but all items leave the company's warehouse within two days of when the orders are placed. As a result, most orders arrive within three to seven days.

After decades as a mail-order company, selling online does present some interesting and sometimes difficult challenges. But they're ones Leblanc and her staff at Harbor Sweets relish. They recognize that the Internet represents the future for their company, and indeed the same is true for many traditional businesses.

4

Building Your Own Web Site

The Lowdown

When most of us think of online retailers, behemoth brands such as Amazon.com, Buy.com, and Overstock.com that sell millions, if not billions, in merchandise every year tend to come to mind. But as this book has shown, your company doesn't have to be huge or heavily capitalized to succeed on the Internet. There are multiple channels for you to sell your products online, including through your own web site. In fact, it has become much less risky than it was previously to hang a shingle online by starting your own e-commerce site.

Online sales are growing at a staggering rate as more consumers gain access to the Internet. At the same time, people are more at ease with shopping online thanks to improvements in security and the proliferation of services like online travel booking, banking, and bill payment. Online sales, including travel, topped $200 billion in 2006, growing by about 20 percent over the previous year, according to *The 2006 State of Retailing Online* report by Shop.org and Forrester Research,

Inc. Those figures are even more significant when you look at them in a historical context. Annual online sales totaled only half that amount just three years earlier.

These statistics underscore the fact that plenty of opportunities still exist for entrepreneurs to build their own successful online businesses. And you're no longer locked into selling through existing marketplaces like Yahoo! Or eBay. It's now possible for an upstart company (or a bricks-and-mortar business wanting to expand into online channels) to build an e-commerce site and begin attracting paying customers immediately. This book is chock-full of examples of companies that have done precisely that.

Some of the largest and fastest-growing segments of online shopping seem tailor-made for upstarts and small companies seeking to specialize in a specific niche. Online sales of pet supplies and cosmetics and fragrances grew by an estimated 30 percent in 2006, more than any other categories, according to the Shop.org/Forrester Research report. Other lucrative merchandise categories are computer hardware and software (with online sales of $16.8 billion); automobiles and auto parts ($15.9 billion); and apparel, accessories, and footwear ($13.8 billion).

Read on to learn more about how to go about building an e-commerce web site while avoiding common perils and mistakes that could derail the process and cost valuable sales.

Getting Started

The whole process of building your own web site is very similar to building a bricks-and-mortar store. First, you've got to secure the real estate, then develop a blueprint, and finally build the store. Most likely, you'll need to bring in experts—be it contractors or skilled employees—to help with construction. Before opening day, you'll need to invest in things like shopping carts, payment-processing technology, and a security system to protect your merchandise and customers. You'll also need to focus on merchandising and make decisions about how products will be showcased and how customers will shop in your store.

As in real life, location, location, location is important on the Internet. As soon as you decide to open an online store, you need to secure a Web address by registering a domain name with Network Solutions or one of the other companies offering this service. Given the proliferation of web sites, you may not be able to register your first-choice dot-com address. Even so, it's important to choose a domain name that will be easy for your customers to remember and type into their browsers. Be wary of URLs that include hard-to-spell words or that could easily be confused with another company's site. In fact, you may want to register variations of your name, so that if someone misspells it, abbreviates it, or adds punctuation, they'll still find your site. You may also want to register the .com, .net, and .biz versions of your web site, too, which again will make it easier for customers to find you. The cost is minimal considering the benefit you'll get from the investment. Also, make sure to register your domain for several years or set up the automatic renewal feature so you don't lose your Web address down the road.

You'll then have to find a company to host your site. Hosting companies essentially rent you disk space on their computers so your site always remains up and running. Some Internet service providers offer hosting packages to their customers, as do many of the domain-registration sites. Some Web developers offer hosting services to their clients as an added service. When choosing a host for your site, consider not only the monthly cost but also your bandwidth allowance and your allotted Web storage space. Don't sign up for a plan without first confirming that the host company can handle the volume of traffic you expect your site to generate. Be sure to find out about reliability and downtimes; as an e-commerce store, you can't afford too many outages. For online help in finding the best host for your web site, visit HostChart.Com at www.HostChart.com or HostCompare at www.hostcompare.com.

Once you have the location for your online store, you'll need to start creating a blueprint for what the site will actually look like. Don't worry if you don't have the programming skills necessary to actually build the site. The goal of this step is to define your vision of the site. You don't have to go as far as picking the paint colors—in this case the color scheme for your store—but you should have a good idea of what the finished site will look like and how it will function. One good way to home in on this vision is by visiting other web sites, including those that will be your competitors. Prepare a list of your favorite features from these sites. Don't be afraid to dream big; you may discover that you can integrate many of these best practices while still staying within your budget. In addition, you'll want to make note of flaws and mistakes from other e-tailers' sites so you can avoid them on yours.

Some important things to consider at this stage are home page design, content, navigation, how products will be categorized, the checkout process, security protections, and the integration of help or frequently asked questions (FAQs) pages. Only after you have a clear vision of how your Web store will function should you attempt to begin building it. Jumping into the construction phase before plans are completed is a disaster waiting to happen, and a costly disaster at that.

These days, many people have experience with HTML coding and Web programming because they've built personal home pages on the Internet. Based on your own experience and comfort level with the Web, you may feel extremely confident in your ability to build a commercial site. But I caution you to harshly and honestly evaluate your skills before undertaking the construction of an e-commerce web site. Remember that online customers often decide where to buy online based on appearances. No matter what your merchandise niche, your site will be competing with professionally designed ones. In addition, some of the features necessary for a Web store may be outside your expertise unless you're a skilled developer. Finally, you don't want to muck up your site because of your inexperience. If you've ever botched a home repair job and had to call in an expert to fix it, you know that stupid mistakes can sometimes be money pits. Unless you come from a

Web design and development background, it's probably smart to hire a professional to build your e-commerce store.

When hiring a Web developer, it's advisable to set a budget up front or to request a detailed bid. You'll then know exactly what the price does and doesn't include. This is a lesson you could apply in any facet of your business; before hiring someone to do work for you, know exactly what they'll deliver for the price you're paying them.

Most importantly, evaluate the developers' work and work habits before hiring them to build your site. Interview the programmers who will be working directly on your site to make sure they understand your vision and have the skills to execute it. Examine their Web design portfolio to ensure that they have experience building the kind of site you want, and to make sure that you will be happy with the quality of work that they do. It's probably a good idea to hire someone with experience in search-engine optimization, a concept you'll learn about in Chapter 6, as this will help in your later Web marketing efforts.

Talk to the developer's current and former clients as a way of checking references. Ask these references about any challenges they encountered while working with the developer. Find out if the project was finished over budget or beyond the deadline. And, by all means, ask if the client would hire the developer again. If the answer is no, you should probably consider hiring someone else who gets better reviews from past clients.

How It Works

One of the greatest benefits of having your own e-commerce store is autonomy. On your own web site, you're not subject to any arbitrary marketplace rules or required to pay any transactional fees, other than your monthly hosting subscription and expenses associated with online credit-card and payment processing. That's one of the reasons many eBay and Amazon merchants migrate to their own sites; profit margins are generally much higher on items sold through independent web sites.

Having a web site is a great way to build a brand, and you should use your site to convey what your company stands for. Having a web site also frees you to offer additional services and perks to your customers, specifically things that are impossible to do in other online marketplaces. For example, you may choose to start a loyalty program that lets customers earn points toward rewards and discounts with every purchase. On your own site, you can easily sell and redeem gift certificates, and you'll be able to process coupons. These things not only generate consumer goodwill, but they also drive repeat business to your site and that will be crucial to your success.

As a Web store operator, you bear the full burden of driving traffic to your site. As you review traffic numbers for your own site, you'll probably come to realize just how effective eBay, Amazon, and Overstock are at attracting customers. Fortunately, there are strategies you can use to increase visitors at your site. Some, like marketing aggressively to existing customers, have already been discussed elsewhere in this book. But those tactics alone won't guarantee the success of your own Web store. Now, more than ever before, you need to use the many different online marketing channels available to you. Make sure your products are indexed in the major comparison-shopping engines. And immediately begin search-engine marketing and search-engine optimization campaigns, which will help bring customers from Google, Yahoo!, and MSN Search directly to your Web store. Read Chapter 6 for tips and specific techniques that will guarantee that your business receives prominent placement in search results.

Once you establish your own web site, you'll probably come to appreciate all the infrastructure and support that other marketplaces provide, particularly in terms of security and payment processing. Those things are your responsibility now, and they are very important to consumers. Though more people are shopping on the Web, consumers are still reticent to buy from companies that they don't know. The best way to overcome that hurdle is by creating a secure web site that your customers can trust. Contract with a reputable company to provide data encryption, security, and a secure shopping cart for your site, and be sure to promote these protections to your customers. In addition, sign up for some of the third-party verification and rating services, such as VeriSign, buySAFE, BizRate, and thawte. It's important for customers to know that "this is a site that you can trust," says Andy Wang of ZipZoomFly, which has been selling through its own web site for almost a decade.

And no matter what your mother might have told you, it's okay to brag, especially when you're trying to promote a new e-commerce store to customers. Let shoppers know that you have experience selling in other channels and a stellar reputation in those marketplaces. Doing so will provide them with another incentive to buy from you. Link to your feedback ratings on eBay, Amazon, Overstock, and other sites to prove that yours is an ethical business with a reputation for good customer service.

What Sells Best

The Internet is a worldwide marketplace with millions of diverse consumers. As a result, anything sells. Items that you may have struggled to sell in other online marketplaces may move quite well in your own Web store.

In addition, your own store is a great place to experiment with good-selling, but lower-margin, items that you were wary to sell on eBay because of high listing fees. The same goes for high-ticket items. You can advertise them virtually risk-free on your own web site because there are no listing fees. For example, Home Décor Products, Inc., sells a $45,000 copper bathtub at its HomeClick.com web site. The company doesn't sell many of the tubs, but when it does, the profits are great and they go directly into the company's coffers.

As for specific categories that sell well on the Web, look to online shopping studies and surveys for cues. As I mentioned earlier in this chapter, the latest research from Shop.org/Forrester Research indicates that computer hardware and software; autos and auto parts; and apparel, accessories, and footwear are the three biggest merchandise categories in terms of online sales. Music and videos; books; sporting goods; toys and games; flowers, cards, and gifts; and jewelry and luxury items are also lucrative categories, according to the National Retail Federation, while pet supplies and cosmetics and fragrances are fast-growing product lines.

To check out the online viability of a product you'd like to sell, use keyword selector tools from Yahoo! and Google to determine just how Internet users are searching for those products every month. If a keyword shows strong search patterns, then it's likely to be a good seller on the Internet.

Pros and Cons

By opening your own Web store, you can finally free your business from the shackles that restrained it in other marketplaces. You'll also be removing the pickpocket's grip on your wallet now that you no longer have to pay listing fees, transaction fees, and commissions. Most online merchants report that their companies become more profitable after opening a Web store because they no longer have to share a cut of every sale.

But as I pointed out in the previous chapter, there are additional expenses that come with running your own web site—credit-card processing fees, monthly hosting fees, pay-per-click advertising costs, e-mail marketing expenses, ad performance tracking fees, and the like. Just the process of building a web site can be very expensive. Some companies spend five or six figures designing and developing their sites. That sounds like a lot of money, but you really don't want to take shortcuts here.

Perhaps the biggest risk of all is that your web site will fail to attract customers. Hopefully, the tips you've read in this chapter and the lessons you'll learn later about search-engine marketing will help your company avoid such a fate. You can also boost your site by avoiding common Web design mistakes. The best way to do that is by thinking about your customers through every phase of site development. Usability is the most important facet of Web design, according to Jack Whitley of Replacements, Ltd. And he should know. His company's site was ranked as one of the Web's best by *Internet Retailer* magazine, and it brings in about $35 million in sales annually.

Most Internet shoppers aren't impressed by sites incorporating lots of animation, video, and superfluous gimmicks on a web page. They're looking for products, and anything you put in the way of that may send them shopping somewhere else.

You want to make it as easy as possible for customers to find products by having a site that is simple to navigate. When people are shopping online, they like to be able to quickly click from one product to the next.

Give customers multiple ways to find what they're looking for. You'll notice that the best shopping sites sort products into categories. They also allow customers to browse by brand, price, size, and other important attributes. It's always a good idea to provide a search bar in your online store so customers can search by keyword or a specific product name.

Providing customers with the information they need is another facet of usability. Outline policies and answer frequently asked questions on your web site, and make it easy for your customers to contact you (preferably by e-mail and telephone) if they can't find the answers they need there. It's also a good idea to provide online customers a mechanism for leaving feedback or questions. You will learn a lot from the comments they post, and you may even be able to use their feedback later for marketing purposes.

With foresight and proper planning, you can avoid the pitfalls and savor the joys of being proprietor of your own Web store. This may be one of the hardest channels to break into, but it also one of the most rewarding.

Action Plan

Here's how to go about building your own web site:

- ✔ If you're new to online commerce, you may want to establish your-self first by selling in one of the other channels, like eBay.

- ✔ Register a domain name for your online store. Make sure to pick one that is easy to remember and spell. Register any variations of the name, as well.

- ✔ Visit other online stores and keep a list of things you like and don't like about each. Also make note of the companies that designed your favorite sites.

- ✔ Develop an outline that you will follow in the design of your Web store. This is the time to plan out the site navigation and determine what types of content you want to include.

- ✔ Begin interviewing Web design and development firms. Make sure they understand exactly how you expect your site to function. Talk to the actual people who will be working on your site, look at their portfolios, and check their references. Request a detailed bid that fully outlines the work the Web development company will perform and the deadlines for completion of each task.

- ✔ If your developer doesn't provide hosting, find another company that can host your site. Make sure you will have adequate bandwidth and storage space to run your business.

- ✔ Begin compiling the content for your site. This includes your prod-uct catalog, any customer guides, and FAQs.

- ✔ Make sure you are enabled to accept online payments by establish-ing a PayPal account and a merchant account with a bank, so you can accept credit card orders.

- ✔ Bolster the security of your site by purchasing a secure shopping cart and data encryption services from reputable companies in the field. In addition, sign up for third-party verification and rating services that convey to customers that yours is a reputable and trustworthy site.

- ✔ As soon as your web site is live, promote it with the search engines and comparison-shopping sites so potential customers can easily find it.

Web Site Success Story

Replacements, Ltd.

When you hate your job, you have to find some other way to have fun. Stuck in a not very satisfying career as a state auditor, Bob Page found his release in antiquing. On the weekends, he'd wake up early, hop into his van, and start hitting yard sales and antique shops in search of complete and mismatched sets of china.

Pretty soon, friends were asking Page to be on the lookout for some piece or another, maybe an extra place setting to complete their wedding registry or a new sugar bowl to replace the one that got broken on the way from the china cabinet to the table. Page wrote each special request on an index card and toted the cards along on his weekend shopping trips. Before long, his hobby morphed into a business, as more people asked Page to find replacement china pieces for them. Page moonlighted for almost three years, spending his weekends on the road and selling china out of his attic, before finally quitting his day job to go into business for himself.

That was on March 17, 1981—nearly three decaades ago—and it's probably one of the smartest moves Page ever made. Back then people thought he was crazy to give up a good job with the state to pursue what certainly seemed them like a harebrained business idea. In fact, he couldn't even get a loan to fund his new business—something the bankers probably regret now. Page started out with just $4,000 in inventory and a similar cushion in the bank.

His company, Replacements, Ltd., is now the world's largest purveyor of replacement and hard-to-find china, silverware, crystal, and collectibles with an in-stock inventory of more than 10 million pieces in more than 200,000 patterns. Many of the items the company sells have been discontinued and aren't available anywhere else but flea markets, garage sales, and eBay. What began as a local business, little more than a favor to friends, quickly expanded to become a nationally known mail-order venture. Now, Replacements is a big-time Web re-tailer with the Internet driving about half of its $75 million in annual sales. Online orders come primarily from the Replacements, Ltd., web site at www.replacements.com, but the company also does business on eBay and Amazon.

Replacements launched its own web site in 1998, but with no e-commerce functionality. The original site was just eight pages long. It offered a bit of the company's background and explained the types of products available. The site also included a place where customers could request a brochure or sign up to receive a listing of the company's inventory for a particular china pattern. About 1,900 people visited the site that first month, most of them directed there by the small ads Replacements ran in the classified sections of *Better Homes and Gardens*, *Southern Living*, and other home magazines.

At the time, no one was quite certain what role, if any, the Internet would play in Replacements' future success. "We weren't sure what e-commerce meant for our business," says Jack Whitley, the company's vice president of e-commerce. "It sounds crazy to say this now, but back in 1998, we weren't sure that our demographic—middle-aged females with high discretionary income—was going to be on the Web."

Sure, other companies were investing millions of dollars to be online. But no one knew whether Replacements, operating in such a niche, needed to do the same. Page and others debated the company's Web strategy and decided to take a tentative and frugal approach by building the site in-house and funding it with profits from the business. "We basically had to bootstrap the site," Whitley says. "It had to pay for itself as we built it." Because of that, Replacements' Web team monitored traffic from the very start to determine if a bigger investment in the web site was warranted. The answer came once Whitley bought a banner advertising campaign on Yahoo! Those initial search-engine ads had a tremendous impact, driving about 200 to 300 potential customers to the Replacements web site every day. Now, some two million people visit the site every month. Since Replacements debuted on the Internet in 1998, its web site has driven more than $150 million in sales.

In building an e-commerce-enabled web site, Replacements concentrated on eight main areas: technical development or programming, content, online marketing, customer relationship management, usability, e-mail, analysis, and design and layout. "Of those eight categories, usability is the most important," Whitley says. "If you want a successful Web effort, the site has to be designed from the customer perspective. People do not come to your web site to be wowed. It's not experiential. They're looking for information and it has to be very easy to find."

Particularly challenging for Replacements was figuring out how to put its vast inventory online in an easy-to-navigate and searchable format. Luckily, the company already had a robust database cataloging every item in inventory, and it was able to transfer that to the Web.

Here, an explanatory segue is necessary. Most modern china is marked on the back with a stamp that includes both the manufacturer's name and pattern name. In those cases, it's very easy for Replacements to help customers find pieces to complete their sets. Match the manufacturer, match the name, then sell the product. But as he built his business, Page quickly discovered that many early manufacturers were not diligent about signing and marking their china. How could he sell those unidentifiable patterns? And how could he sell to customers who didn't know their pattern name?

Page decided to build a database of every unique pattern in his inventory, to make identifying and selling unmarked pieces easier. Each pattern is cataloged with a photograph and by various attributes, including shape, color, pattern details, and other distinguishing features. So, even if customers don't know their pattern name, Page can match it to items in his inventory.

The Replacements web site includes inventory listings and photographs for more than 200,000 items. Customers navigate by first choosing the manufacturer and then selecting the pattern from an alphabetized list. Product detail pages include an image of the pattern and a listing of pieces Replacements has in that pattern. If Replacements doesn't have the particular piece a customer is looking for, the customer can request that Replacements find the product and notify them when it comes in stock. There's nothing fancy about how Replacements indexes its products on the Web. In fact, visually the web site is quite plain. But it is easy to navigate and items can be found easily. "With all our inventory, we knew one of our challenges was to help somebody come into the site and easily browse for their pieces," Whitley says. "We have worked very hard to make it as easy to use with the breadth and depth that we carry."

The Replacements.com web site, which is comprised of more than 300,000 separate pages, is optimized for customers with dial-up Internet access and therefore has few graphics. Images are compressed to load quickly so shoppers don't have to wait for the computer to catch up with them. Whitley is concerned with how quickly pages load, almost to the point of obsession. "If the site is not fast, there is an absolute cost associated with that," he says. "I'm talking a 12-second page load versus three."

In total, Replacements spent less than $250,000 building its e-commerce site, and the company continues to invest in the online channel mainly with marketing and advertising initiatives. Through Yahoo!'s Overture network and Google's AdWords, the company bids on more than 120,000 different keywords and spends several million dollars annually on paid-search campaigns. Because of the sheer volume, Replacements has outsourced management of its keyword advertising campaigns to Efficient Frontier. In the first year of the partnership, paid search-driven sales increased more than 30 percent. Without help from Efficient Frontier, Replacements would not be able to manage such a high number of keyword ads, Whitley says, and conversion ratios would likely be lower.

To further drive traffic to its web site, Replacements maintains a presence on a variety of comparison-shopping engines, including Froogle, Shopping.com, BizRate, and Yahoo! Shopping. Every three weeks, the company feeds its entire catalog to Froogle because it's free to list there. On those shopping engines that charge a commission for every click, Replacements posts only its best-selling items to control marketing costs.

Finally, Replacements has seller accounts with eBay and Amazon. The company opened its Amazon storefront at www.amazon.com/replacements in 2004 after two years of negotiations and preparations. Chiefly, Replacements had to invest in a "prohibitively expensive" system upgrade that allowed its computer servers to communicate with Amazon's and provide real-time inventory information to the e-tailer. The partnership gives Replacements exposure to a new and broader audience of customers, but sales on Amazon account for only a small fraction of revenues. "After two years, we are still outselling them 40 to 1 on our site," Whitley says.

EBay is perhaps the biggest competitor that Replacements faces on the Web. At any given time, the site hosts more than 120,000 auctions in the china and dinnerware category. Rather than being cowed by the competition, Replacements has embraced it by opening its own eBay store and staging auctions there. Replacements, selling under the user ID replacementsltd, has about 30,000 items for sale through auction or fixed price at eBay. (Replacements even buys products on eBay to stock in its own inventory.)

The products that Replacements lists on eBay generally are popular, best-selling items, as opposed to rare and hard-to-find pieces. The reasoning is simple. The advantage of being on eBay is to tap into the site's huge audience, and the best way to do that is by offering products that lots of people will come searching for. While eBay is a lucrative channel for Replacements, it pales compared to the company's web site. For that reason, Page and Whitley don't fret too much about the financial impact of eBay on their Internet business. They also realize that the smaller sellers on eBay can't compete with Replacements in terms of reputation, selection, and service.

"If you aggregate all the small shops on eBay, we have a lot of competition out there," Whitley observes. "But we're going to offer things that can't be found on eBay—all the pieces in a pattern grouped together. We have 25 years in business and a 30-day, no-questions-asked, money-back guarantee. If you needed six pieces of Noritake, on eBay you'd have to buy from different sellers."

Replacements has certainly made an amazing climb in the last quarter century, rocketing from $159,000 in revenues that first year to about $75 million in 2006. The company has never had an unprofitable year, and the financials keep getting better as Replacements harnesses the power of the Internet to attract customers and drive sales.

Web Site Success Story

Organic Bouquet

When Gerald Prolman went into business for himself, he did more than establish an online retailer. He created a new industry.

Prolman, who has worked in the natural and organic products industry since the late 1970s, began formulating a plan to start an online organic floral business in 2000. At the time, there were no organic floral suppliers and there didn't appear to be the groundswell of consumer demand for organic flowers, as there was for organic foods.

"Back then, there were already upscale natural food supermarkets and stores promoting natural products, waving the green flag," Prolman says. Most of these stores had high-end floral departments. "I didn't notice anything ecological about the floral departments. People didn't realize—or ask the question—about how the flowers were grown," he adds. "There was this assumption when you walked into a store that promoted sustainably grown products, that mission carried on throughout all departments. That was not the case in flowers. I wanted to start a business that would generate positive social and environmental change, and saw organic flowers as a category that had been completely overlooked."

Prolman persisted with his plan, driven by his own intuition and desire to do good in the world. "When I started this business, there was basically no supply and no demand and no money," he says.

Before he could even think about launching his company, Organic Bouquet, online, Prolman had to create a supply chain of organically grown flowers. He traveled to South America and signed contracts with farmers there, guaranteeing them a certain price for every organic flower they grew for him. Since then, Organic Bouquet has helped convert more than 20,000 acres in five countries to organic farmland, and the company now also works with growers in California and Oregon.

Prolman is no stranger to the organic industry, having founded the fresh-product vendor Made In Nature, a company he sold in 1994 to Dole Food Company. He first became enamored with organic farming techniques in 1989 after visiting a family-owned organic farm. "The grower explained to me how he went about producing his crop organically," Prolman says. "I had never thought about how crops were grown before, nor that there was quite an artillery of chemicals used to produce crops. When I found out how crops were grown and the alternative organic method, I was smitten by the concept, and just taken by the question of why all crops aren't grown this way."

Flowers were, therefore, a natural progression. Working with South American farms, Organic Bouquet produced its first crop of organic tulips in 2002. But without year-round supplies, Prolman couldn't launch his online floral site just yet. So, he started out by selling the flowers to Whole Foods Markets, Wild Oat Markets, Trader Joe's, and other natural and organic food retailers. This was an early way to educate environmentally conscious consumers about the benefits of buying organically grown flowers. By Valentine's Day 2004, the company, which is based in Mill Valley, California, had launched its own web site at www.organicbouquet.com.

In addition to all the normal challenges inherent with starting an online business, Prolman faced the further obstacle of convincing and educating consumers about the benefits of organically grown flowers compared to conventionally grown ones.

"The basic message of organics is that this is an environmental farming method," Prolman says. "Organic at its core is about the farming, not necessarily about the foods."

Smartly, Organic Bouquet targeted its initial marketing efforts to consumers who were already buying organic products and whose concerns about the environment shaped their buying habits. These are what the industry refers to as lifestyles of health and sustainability (LOHAS) consumers. Some 63 million Americans spend $230 billion annually on socially and environmentally responsible products, whether it's fair-trade coffee, hybrid vehicles, ethanol fuel, solar heating panels, recycled blue jeans, or natural cosmetics. These consumers also happen to be affluent and educated, which increases the likelihood that they will shop and make purchases online. Organic Bouquet is the only online florist providing an alternative for them.

Organic Bouquet's own sales figures and the continued growth of the organic industry in the United States seem to prove that Prolman's hunch was right. Organic Bouquet sold an estimated $5 million worth of merchandise in 2006, up from $3 million the previous year. Meanwhile, the U.S. organic industry continues to grow at a double digit rate. Within the nonfood category, organic flowers have been experiencing the most dramatic increase in sales.

A team of in-house developers known as the Boxing Frogs spent five months designing and programming Organic Bouquet's web site. The goal from the beginning was to position Organic Bouquet as "the destination for high-quality, long-lasting flowers that help senders say, 'I care about you and the earth, too,'" Prolman said.

As a new brand on the Internet, Prolman notes, it was essential that Organic Bouquet's online store communicate integrity by displaying commonly recognized certifications for its industry—specifically the U.S. Department of Agriculture Organic seal, the Veriflora green-label certification for the floral industry, the Biodynamics seal that indicates the company and its suppliers practice sustainable agriculture, and the Fair Trade Certified logo that indicates Organic Bouquet pays a fair price for its goods. In addition, Prolman tasked his Web team with focusing on those things that are important for any e-commerce site—reliability, quality depictions of products, and easy-to-use navigation. "What we're selling is integrity, reliability, and quality," he says.

To help convert online flower buyers to Organic Bouquet, the company prices its products competitively and charges just $12.95 for UPS overnight shipping to any destination within the United States, even though the actual shipping cost may be higher. "We're subsidizing the difference," Prolman says, because the company's internal research has shown that higher shipping charges cause people to abandon their online shopping carts. "One of the best things you can do to increase your conversions is to add free shipping. We can't afford to do that. We looked at various data and found that $12.95 was kind of a threshold."

Organic Bouquet also offers a seven-day vase life guarantee on all its flowers. If the blooms don't last for seven days, Organic Bouquet will issue a refund or replacement. The company rarely has to make good on that guarantee, Prolman says, because its flowers tend to last longer than seven days thanks to variety selection, post-harvest care, and cold-chain management. "By taking care of those things, we can add days to the vase life without using chemical preservatives," Prolman adds.

To help boost profits, Organic Bouquet uses cross-selling techniques to boost incremental sales. At checkout, customers are offered the option of adding additional products, such as a recycled green glass vase, organic chocolates, a spa gift set, or a teddy bear stuffed with dried organic lavender, to their bouquet orders.

Organic Bouquet has taken a unique approach to cultivating customers for its web sites. In addition to traditional search-engine marketing campaigns, which bring in about 30 percent of revenues, the company partners with nonprofits to drive traffic to its site. Charitable organizations such as Amnesty International, People for the Ethical Treatment of Animals (PETA), the American Red Cross, Women for Women, the National Wildlife Federation, Heifer International, Adopt-A-Minefield, and many others promote Organic Bouquet flowers to their membership base, in much the same way that online affiliates do.

These charities get a cut of every sale they refer. "We are reaching people who passionately care about social justice, the environment, and animal rights," Prolman says. "Everybody wins in that equation. We're making money by helping charities, and the people buying the flowers feel good." Organic Bouquet has marketing agreements with two dozen nonprofits, and that number continues to grow. Such affiliate deals account for 20 percent of the company's revenues.

Organic Bouquet has similar marketing agreements with companies like ice cream maker Ben & Jerry's, where it is the preferred in-house florist. The company has linked up with other businesses, as well, to secure placement on corporate intranet systems. That way when workers give flowers, they buy directly from Organic Bouquet instead of one of its nonorganic competitors. A new wholesale web site is attempting to win the flower business of hotels, spas, restaurants, and religious institutions and also aims to tap into the huge bridal market. Organic Bouquet even has a partnership with United Airlines, where frequent-flier club members can trade in their miles for flowers.

In addition, the company markets directly to existing customers to cultivate repeat sales. When someone places an order for the first time at Organic Bouquet, the customer is prompted to enroll in the Eco-Points Rewards Program and to sign up for the company's e-mail newsletter and special offers. Eco-Points equate to cash discounts on products purchased through Organic Bouquet's web site. Consumers earn one point for every dollar spent; once they accumulate 10 points, the points can be redeemed for discounts on purchases. Ten points earn a $1 discount, while 50 points earn a $5 discount. Customers can also save up points for free flowers—300 points buys a $29.95 bouquet and 600 points buys a $59.95 bouquet.

At least once a month, registered users receive a special discount or offer via e-mail. The e-mail offer is usually for a holiday-themed bouquet or a special packaged arrangement available exclusively to existing Organic Bouquet customers. "You will only find out about that through e-mail," Prolman says. Customers also receive a monthly e-mail newsletter that usually includes articles about the company's philosophy or its farming practices and updates about the organic industry. Past newsletters have featured profiles of Organic Bouquet growers, along with stories about the company's cause marketing partners and the work they're doing. Organic Bouquet also uses the newsletters for marketing purposes. The newsletter may include links to specific products and special offers or notices about upcoming promotions. "It's a soft sell," Prolman points out. "There's always something you can buy in the newsletter, but it's not a hit-you-over-the-head sale."

Given that the organic flower market is still in its nascent stages, Organic Bouquet has aggressively touted its story to the media. Prolman works with a West Coast public relations (PR) agency to spread the story of Organic Bouquet. "My last name starts with PR," he jokes. Sending out press releases and pitching stories to publications such as the *Wall Street Journal* and *Entrepreneur* magazine has been an effective and inexpensive way of promoting the Organic Bouquet brand and web site to a wider audience of flower-buying consumers.

"PR has played a significant role in driving people to our site," Prolman says, noting that in just one year the company has been featured in more than 1,000 articles, resulting in more than 50 million impressions. "We needed help to get the message out, and Organic Bouquet is an attractive media story. When you don't have $100 million to spend building an online floral company, you've got to find any way you possibly can to get the word out through low-cost, grassroots marketing initiatives."

5

Other Auction Sites and Online Marketplaces

Through the years, as eBay has increased in popularity and achieved tremendous financial success, a steady stream of competing marketplaces has emerged, hoping to steal market share from the online giant. Some existing Internet companies, such as Yahoo!, Amazon.com, and Overstock.com, have tweaked their business models to allow individuals and businesses to sell on their sites. Then there are the dozens of small, upstart auction sites trying to compete directly with eBay. Like so many other companies of the dot-com era, many of these businesses became mired in debt and unable to turn a profit, and most such sites are now defunct. But there are still a few other auction sites challenging eBay today. These competitors seem to have given up the notion that their sites will be the David that topples eBay's Goliath. Instead, most are promoting themselves as complementary marketplaces, channels where savvy sellers can capture incremental sales and reach a customer base that might not shop on eBay. That's how you should view them, as well.

Among merchants, the general consensus about these other auction sites and marketplaces seems to be this: No other site draws the traffic that eBay does, so many auctions conducted on these platforms may end without resulting in a sale. Revenues aren't as robust as they are on eBay. But because competition among sellers isn't as robust, either, individual items often sell for much higher prices in these other marketplaces, resulting in heftier profit margins.

Michael Jansma's company, GEMaffair, sells through a variety of online channels—its own web sites, eBay, Amazon, Overstock, and PropertyRoom.com. EBay accounts for about 55 percent of the company's sales, which total in the millions of dollars every year. The rest comes from these other marketplaces.

"Success is a matter of perspective. I have success on all of them," Jansma says. "We sell products efficiently on each one. We sell more product on eBay than any other place, but such sales bring in less money [or profit] than what we earn on other sites."

When determining how to divvy up your business among eBay and the other online marketplaces, it's smart to keep a few important statistics in mind: eBay remains the powerhouse of online auction sites. In fact, it ranks as one of the busiest and most trafficked e-commerce sites on the Web. It consistently is one of the top 10 most visited sites on the Web, sitting alongside such search engines as Yahoo!, Google, and MSN Search. In addition, eBay has a broader reach than any of its auction-house competitors, according to Alexa, a company that ranks and analyzes web site traffic. EBay's reach is 3.5 percent, meaning that 35,000 of every 1 million Internet users visit the site.

By comparison, Overstock.com reaches 2,150 of every 1 million Internet users. (This figure includes both the auction and e-commerce sides of the business; only about 8 percent of visitors to the Overstock web site visit its Auctions landing page, according to Alexa.) Other auction sites reach an even smaller audience: uBid reaches 310 of every

1 million Internet users, iOffer reaches 250, Bid4Assets reaches 35, Bidville reaches 25, and PropertyRoom and whaBAM! each reach 15. Despite their smaller size, that doesn't mean these aren't valuable marketplaces. In fact, most successful online entrepreneurs recognize the value of selling in multiple channels, from the smallest marketplaces to the largest, as a way of extending their brand, reaching the broadest possible customer base, and capturing a bigger share of the billions that are spent online every year.

Online consumer auction sales will reach $65 billion by 2010, accounting for nearly one-fifth of all online retail sales, according to the most recent data from Forrester Research. "It's really about ubiquity," says Holly MacDonald-Korth of Overstock.com. "You want to be everywhere someone looks. No matter what web site someone goes to, you want your product available for sale there."

Read on to learn about a few of the top online auction sites and other marketplaces where you successfully can sell your products.

OVERSTOCK AUCTIONS

The Lowdown

Of all the auction sites, Overstock has made the biggest inroads against eBay, largely because the site already had a strong customer base before it launched an auction platform. In addition, Overstock Auctions (www.auctions.overstock.com) has deliberately catered to disgruntled eBay merchants by offering lower fees, better fraud protection, and other solutions to common eBay seller problems and complaints.

Overstock is the Web's ultimate outlet. The company launched in 1999 as an online retailer specializing in the sale of closeout merchandise on the Internet. Since that time, gross merchandise sales have grown from $1.8 million to $868 million. Overstock hooks consumers by offering new, brand-name merchandise at prices 40 percent to 80 percent less than retail. (The average discount is 48 percent, according to Holly MacDonald-Korth, who works in the company's marketing department.)

In September 2004, nine years after the advent of eBay, Overstock entered the online auction business and began allowing outside merchants to offer items for sale on the site. Overstock approached the online auctioneering space with the goal of becoming the low-price leader in the industry. Overstock Auctions initially set its fees 30 percent lower than eBay's. Because of subsequent fee hikes on eBay, it now costs about 40 percent less to sell on Overstock Auctions, according to MacDonald-Korth. Auction insertion fees range from 17 cents to $3.17 on Overstock Auctions. In addition, sellers pay a closing fee of at least 3.25 percent on every item that sells on the site. (By comparison, eBay's insertion fees range from 20 cents to $4.80; the site also charges a closing fee, or final-value fee, of at least 5.25 percent of the selling price.)

Overstock offers subscription-based pricing for sellers who want to control their costs more tightly. Under the various subscription plans, sellers are allowed to post a certain number of auctions every month without paying insertion fees. The plans range from $6.95 for 25 concurrent auctions to $79.95 for 7,500 concurrent auctions. In addition, Overstock takes a 5 percent commission for items sold through a subscription plan. Sellers must also pay a $15 activation fee to set up a subscription, but discounts are offered for those signing on for three, six, or twelve months, and to Overstock Trusted Merchants, Enterprise Merchants, and members of the Trusted Overstock Auction Sellers Affiliate (TOASA).

Getting Started

Before you can sell (or buy) on Overstock Auctions, you need to set up an account. You can begin the registration process at the auction site's home page at www.auctions.overstock.com. You'll be asked to choose a user ID, which will be the handle your customers know you by, and a password so you can access secure information about your account. In addition, you'll need to provide your first and last name, as well as your birth date and billing address. That's the extent of the simple registration process. However, in order to complete transactions on Overstock Auctions, you'll need to become a verified registered user. This involves providing a valid credit card number, which Overstock will attempt to validate by obtaining a $1 authorization on the card. If the authorization is successful, you'll receive an e-mail from Overstock with instructions on how to activate your account.

Once set up as verified registered user, you should take the time to customize your Overstock personal home page, which is sort of like an "About Me" page on eBay where customers can find out more about your business. The home page will include a sampling of five items you're selling, your business rating (Overstock's version of feedback), as well as any additional information you choose to provide, such as shipping, payment, and return policies, along with customized HTML coding. Your personal home page will become an important branding and marketing tool for your online auction business.

When you become eligible to do so, you would be wise to join TOASA, a peer community, and become a Trusted Merchant on Overstock. Doing so will increase your credibility with buyers, and you'll also receive certain discounts on Overstock Auctions fees.

Trusted Merchants must go through a bonding process with buySAFE. The company verifies a seller's identity and runs financial checks to ensure the seller's ability to honor the terms and conditions of any online sales. Shoppers who purchase from a buySAFE-approved Trusted Merchant have an added measure of security against fraud and unethical business practices. When a shopper buys from a Trusted Merchant, buySAFE's surety partner Liberty Mutual guarantees the transaction up to $25,000. If the seller does not meet any of the terms of sale, the buyer can get a replacement item or a refund up to $25,000. Sellers must be based in the United States, have three months of experience doing business online, and $1,000 in monthly sales before they can seek Trusted Merchant status and bonding through buySAFE.

Becoming a Trusted Merchant will also get your auctions more prominence in Overstock's search results. When someone searches for an item on the main Overstock shopping site, only auctions offered by Trusted Merchants show up in the search results. This gives you an opportunity to entice Overstock's regular retail customers to buy from you at auction.

About half of all items for sale at Overstock Auctions are offered by Trusted Merchants. Statistics suggest that going through the buySAFE bonding process can improve sellers' revenues and increase the number of transactions on the auction site. According to J.T. Stephens, assistant vice president of auctions for Overstock, the average Trusted Merchant sees completed sales jump by about 83 percent within one month of joining the program. "One month prior to becoming a Trusted Merchant, they average 120 sales per month," he says. "One month after, they average 220 sales."

Becoming a TOASA member will also give you credibility with bidders—and you'll be eligible for certain discounts on Overstock fees. As with the Trusted Merchant program, sellers must have a proven track record before being accepted for membership in TOASA. Applicants must have three months of recent selling history on Overstock Auctions, and they must maintain at least 20 listings per month on the site. In addition, applicants are required to have a rating of 20 or more from unique buyers and a minimum positive ratings percentage before they're accepted for TOASA membership.

How It Works

If you've auctioned off items on eBay, you should have no difficulty selling on the Overstock Auctions platform. As with eBay, Overstock Auctions sellers have the ability to customize their auctions with photographs and such listing enhancements as bold or highlighted text. Sellers can list items for sale in multiple categories to capture the attention of more potential bidders. They are also able to choose to feature an item (for an additional fee) so it appears earlier in listings, set a reserve price, or give buyers the option of circumventing the bidding process through an option called "Make It Mine," similar to eBay's Buy It Now option. As a way to rein in fraud, Overstock Auctions makes this option available only to sellers with a business rating of 10 or higher.

As a seller, you have the option of listing your items manually, using a step-by-step seller interface tool on Overstock's web site. Or you may bulk list items using auction management software, including O-Lister (Overstock's auction management tool), ChannelAdvisor, Meridian, Zoovy, Infopia, Truition, Auction Wizard, Marketworks, Kyozou, and ChannelMax.

As with eBay, the seller decides how long an item remains on the auction block. At Overstock, you'll be able to choose an auction duration of either three, five, seven, or ten days. Unlike with eBay, however, you won't be able to dictate to the minute how long an auction lasts. That's because Overstock auctions automatically extend for an additional 10 minutes anytime a bid is received within 10 minutes of the scheduled closing time. This is done specifically to discourage sniping, a last-minute bidding practice that has becoming increasingly popular—and frustrating—on eBay.

"We wanted to give consumers the option to really win an item that they want," MacDonald-Korth says. She notes that this feature is popular with both buyers and sellers. Auctions that extend end up with a 20 percent higher closing price than those that don't, she adds.

Sellers have the choice of receiving payment for their auctions in a variety of ways—including PayPal, personal check, or money order. They can also opt to receive credit card payments using the site's O-Auctions Checkout system. Sellers choosing this option are required to pay a per-transaction fee.

As with eBay and many other online marketplaces, feedback from buyers and sellers drives transactions. Overstock Auctions has two separate feedback systems—business ratings and personal ratings. Of those, your business rating has the biggest impact on your bottom line and determines whether people feel comfortable bidding on your auctions. (Personal ratings do not affect your business ratings score.)

Once two users have completed a transaction, they're given the opportunity to rate the other party by offering two thumbs up, one thumb up, one thumb down and one thumb up, one thumb down, or two thumbs down. Overstock uses these assessments to calculate a numerical business ratings score for every buyer and seller. That number is prominently displayed in every auction the seller posts, and it's also visible in search listings so bidders can easily compare the scores of various sellers. In addition to the numerical business rating, Overstock calculates a positive ratings percentage for each buyer and seller. This figure gives bidders an idea of a seller's track record by indicating the percentage of transactions resulting in a favorable rating.

What Sells Best

Because Overstock is foremost a shopping site, it has a slightly different demographic pattern than many online auction sites. According to Hitwise, more than half of the site's visitors (60 percent) are female. The biggest cluster of Overstock shoppers are women aged 25 to 44 years old. Elsewhere on the Internet, however, men are more likely to participate in online auctions. A wide-ranging look at how men and women use the Internet by the Pew Internet & American Life Project showed that 30 percent of male Internet users had participated in online auctions, compared to just 18 percent of women.

Given those statistics, it's no surprise that merchandise categories that appeal to female shoppers are among the most popular on Overstock Auctions. In order of popularity, those include jewelry and watches; clothing, shoes, and accessories; and home and garden. Other popular items are those that have mass appeal regardless of gender, such as computer equipment, mobile phones, and DVDs and movies.

As important as having the right product in a hot category is pricing and marketing that product appropriately. Because the audience of customers is smaller on Overstock Auctions, it's critical to adopt a pricing strategy that fits the marketplace. In the eBay chapter, you read about how some sellers start every auction at 99 cents, even on very valuable items. They're able to price things that way because eBay attracts millions of shoppers who ratchet up demand for these 99-cent items and drive up the price. But the same thing doesn't always happen at Overstock or the other smaller auction sites where traffic is lower.

When Overstock Auctions was in its nascent stages, company officials actually warned sellers not to list their items for sale for too much below market value. They were concerned auctions wouldn't attract enough bidders to drive the price up and that sellers would lose money. That isn't necessarily the case now that the auction side of the business is more robust, MacDonald-Korth says. In fact, some of the site's most successful merchants practice the 99-cent pricing strategy. It's important to note, however, that most of these merchants deal in very popular items with high demand, such as electronics. "We've got one merchant who sells basically all iPods with a starting bid of around $1. About 98 percent of his auctions end up closing for close to the manufacturer's suggested retail price," she says.

Unless you're selling a sure thing, like iPods, there's a real danger to setting opening bid prices too low. You could end up giving away expensive merchandise to low bidders, effectively decimating your profit margin and firebombing your business. Therefore, it's best to take a more measured approach to pricing on Overstock. You can guarantee that all of your sales will be profitable by setting the opening bid price on every item at slightly above cost, including any transaction fees. To improve your sell-through rate—the percentage of auctions that end in a sale—and minimize your auction fees, consider signing up for a subscription-pricing plan on Overstock. And always study the marketplace carefully. Unless you can offer a significantly lower price than your competitors, don't list an item if there are too many other similar ones for sale on the site. Wait until the marketplace is less crowded. Follow the same reasoning when doing your own inventory planning. Don't compete with yourself. If you have multiple quantities of the same item, slowly leak them onto the marketplace over a period of weeks or months. A buyer's perception of scarcity drives sales and drives prices up.

uBID

The Lowdown

Founded 10 years ago, uBid promotes itself as the "marketplace that you can trust" because all of the merchandise for sale on the site comes either directly from uBid itself or from third-party merchants who have been financially vetted and verified. UBid has erected these barriers to entry in an attempt to create a fraud-free marketplace where shoppers can feel comfortable bidding without fear of being ripped off financially or receiving stolen or counterfeit goods. As on Amazon, all payments are made directly to uBid, which then pays sellers—meaning that buyers don't have to share credit card numbers or other financial details with the site's independent merchants.

Traffic on uBid is strong compared to the other smaller auction sites, but it pales in comparison with eBay. UBid has 5 million registered users compared to eBay's more than 200 million. The site attracts 2 million visitors every month, about the same number of people who visit eBay every day. In its 10-year history, uBid and its certified merchants have sold more than $1 billion worth of merchandise through the site, a tiny fraction of what is sold on eBay annually. Despite these disparities, online merchants pursuing a multichannel approach and looking for the widest exposure for their products should consider joining the uBid marketplace. It's a particularly valuable place to sell if you market high-ticket items or sell in categories where fraud or counterfeiting is rampant.

Getting Started

Before you can sell on uBid, you must complete the site's registration process. You'll be asked to do much more than choose a user ID and provide a credit card number. Before you're able to list goods for sale, uBid merchants must pass a 10-point approval process. Depending on how crowded a particular marketplace is, your application to sell on the site may not be accepted. For example, uBid recently wasn't accepting any more watch merchants.

Clearly uBid isn't a marketplace for newcomers. You'll need to have experience as a seller and a proven track record as a reputable, honest business before being certified to sell on the site. In fact, the uBid Certified Merchant program was created to cater to small and medium-sized business sellers. More than 900 sellers are currently enrolled in the program.

With your application, you'll be asked to submit a tax identification number or Social Security number, along with a valid credit card number and bank account information (specifically your checking and savings account numbers). UBid also asks for the names of three business references, such as suppliers, vendors, and bankers, who can vouch for your ethics and financial stability. The auction site obtains a Dun & Bradstreet report for each applicant and asks for details about what you plan to sell on uBid, your company's annual gross revenues, and the number of people you employ.

UBid's checks go even further. Before being allowed to sell certain brands on the site, you'll need to show proof that your company is an authorized dealer of those products. Beyond the vetting process, uBid employs a variety of checks and balances to ensure sellers' legitimacy and the quality of goods they're offering for sale. The company randomly purchases products from its own Certified Merchants to make sure everything is aboveboard. UBid also deals directly with customer service problems and becomes involved in merchant-buyer disputes.

How It Works

Although the marketplace is clearly modeled after eBay, uBid is a unique player in the online auction space. It is, in a sense, a hybrid of Amazon and eBay. UBid is a retailer, dealing in new, closeout, overstock, and refurbished merchandise from distributors and manufacturers, but the marketplace is also open to other merchants. Though it allows third-party sellers, uBid assumes much tighter control over those transactions than Overstock does. Depending on your perspective as a seller, that may be a good or bad thing.

For example, uBid may require sellers to offer a 30-day return policy on items sold through the site. As mentioned earlier, all payments for auctions (or fixed-price uBuyitnow purchases) are made directly via credit card to uBid, which then distributes the funds to the seller. And uBid staffs a customer service center (available online and by telephone) to take buyers' questions about products and resolve any disputes between merchants and bidders. Some sellers may welcome the ability to pass along payment processing and time-consuming customer service tasks to someone else. But others may be wary of abdicating control of such an important part of their business, as exemplary customer service is often a way that merchants brand themselves and stand out from the competition.

Unlike other marketplaces, uBid offers sellers few opportunities to brand themselves before making a sale. Auction ads include all the pertinent information about the item being sold, including a description and photography. Bidders are informed whether the item is being offered by uBid directly or by a third-party Certified Merchant. But they don't learn exactly who the seller is until after the sale.

There are a few other features that differentiate uBid from eBay and its other competitors. First, forget about insertion fees. UBid doesn't charge Certified Merchants anything to list items for auction or for sale at a fixed price. However, merchants pay dearly on the back end when an item sells, anywhere from 2.5 percent of the closing price on goods selling for $1,001 or more to 12.5 percent of the closing price of goods selling for $25 or less. Because there are no insertion fees, uBid merchants can run auctions for longer than 10 days. And like Overstock, uBid discourages sniping by extending an auction if any bids are received within the final 10 minutes. The auction will keep extending until there are no bids for 10 continuous minutes, and there's no limit to the number of times a uBid auction can be extended.

Finally, uBid maintains stricter rules for bidders than other auction sites. Before shoppers can bid on an item at uBid, they must register and submit a valid, verifiable credit card to prove that they're serious, qualified buyers. The site and its Certified Merchants ship products only to U.S. addresses, and buyers aren't allowed to back out of a transaction by canceling a bid. These requirements are attempts by uBid to reduce fraud.

Sellers shouldn't look to uBid as a way of building repeat business or driving customers to their own branded site. Instead, treat it as an additional revenue stream and a platform where you may be able to squeeze out bigger profit margins because of the high trust level between buyers and sellers.

What Sells Best

Before launching its third-party auction service, uBid carved out a niche for itself as a retailer of computers and electronics, with a focus on refurbished and soon-to-be discontinued items. Those same items continue to dominate the site and tend to be the best sellers, along with other electronics goods, like digital cameras, televisions, cell phones, and accessories. You'll also find heavy bidding for fine jewelry products, where many auctions commence at $1. Additional merchandise for sale on uBid fits into one of six other categories: apparel; home and garden; sports; collectibles; music, movies, and games; and travel.

While computers, jewelry, and electronics are hot on eBay, most customers aren't making high-ticket purchases at uBid. Bargain shoppers are attracted by the uBid promise that many items on the site can be purchased for 20 percent to 80 percent below retail prices. The average order value for items sold by uBid Certified Merchants is in the $100 range, according to company financial reports filed with the U.S. Securities and Exchange Commission. Sellers therefore will do best marketing affordable items on the web site.

In many instances on uBid, sellers list multiple quantities of the same item for sale simultaneously and give buyers the option to buy the item immediately or duke it out in an auction. For instance, a Certified Merchant recently offered 20 Magellan GPS devices. Bidding started at $1, but shoppers also had the option of buying the item outright for $349. At the end of the auction, any remaining GPS devices not snapped up by uBuyitnow customers were sold to the top bidders at various prices. During the bidding process, shoppers get to see how many items have been purchased at the uBuyitnow price and what other bidders are willing to pay for the remaining quantity. This helps them decide how much to bid so they don't miss out on the chance to purchase. This transparent bidding process fuels competition among bidders and increases the likelihood that items will sell for the uBuyitnow price or higher.

iOFFER

The Lowdown

IOffer is one of the Web's most heavily trafficked trading communities, despite maintaining a relatively low profile and shunning publicity. IOffer is routinely compared to other auction sites, but that definition doesn't quite fit. Instead, it's more like a virtual flea market where the person who makes the best offer walks away with the goods. The company bills itself as a peer-to-peer negotiation site, where buyers and sellers barter and haggle until they agree on a price for an item. It's classified advertising gone high tech, and it may be the best place to sell items of uncertain value or those that haven't sold in other online channels.

At the iOffer web site at www.ioffer.com, you'll find items for sale in more than two dozen categories, including antiques and art, photos, books, electronics, hobbies and crafts, computers, toys and games, and various collectibles. But unlike most other auction sites, bids (or offers, as they're referred to on iOffer) drive the price down, not up. If that seems confusing to you, think of what happens at flea markets. IOffer is built around haggling; the idea is for a buyer and seller to find a compromise price that makes them both happy. Shoppers at iOffer can certainly agree to pay a seller's initial asking price for an item, but the marketplace encourages buyers to make offers as a way of setting their own price for goods. And, in the spirit of negotiation, sellers are allowed to make counteroffers and negotiate simultaneously with multiple people to get the most money for their merchandise.

Getting Started

To get started selling on iOffer, you'll need to register on the site and choose a user ID. In order to be able to sell, you'll need to provide a valid credit card number or send in a $20 deposit (via PayPal or check or money order) to cover any selling fees you accrue. The second step is setting up a personal profile page. This is not required, but it's recommended because it will provide potential buyers with information about your business and the items you'll be selling on iOffer.

Finally, you'll want to take action to boost your reputation on iOffer. The site has its own feedback system that allows buyers and sellers to rate one another after a transaction. But you don't have to wait until you have a few sales under your belt to beef up that rating. IOffer allows its users to aggregate their feedback from other online marketplaces, including eBay, Yahoo!, Overstock, Bidville, and Sell.com using a downloadable tool called Mr. Grabber. (You can find the download link for Mr. Grabber at www.ioffer.com/mrgrabber/.) Once you download Mr. Grabber and launch the program, you'll be prompted to enter your eBay ID and password, as well as your iOffer ID and password, to initiate the transfer of your feedback score to iOffer. (To import feedback from other sites, you can use the similar Web Grabber tool at www.ioffer.com/webgrabber.do to bring in your ratings in just one click.) Though you're a newbie to the iOffer platform, you won't look like one to potential buyers, and that will increase the likelihood that your items will sell at the price you want for them.

How It Works

Once you've completed those few steps, you're ready to start selling. Listing items for sale is essentially risk-free because iOffer charges a fee only if you come to terms with a buyer and agree to sell. What's more, if you list more than two items, iOffer will give you a free online store where you can showcase all your merchandise.

As noted, iOffer is a negotiation site, not an auction site. So, as a seller, you have several ways of marketing your products to potential buyers. The easiest way—and the one that offers the most exposure— is to post an online classified ad describing your item and indicating your asking price. During the listing process, you choose the category in which to list your item; listing in a second category costs an extra 10 cents. You're also given the option of including up to six photographs (the first one is free, and additional ones cost 5 cents each) and jazzing up your ad with highlighted ($2 extra) or bold ($1 extra) text. If you really want to improve your ad's visibility, you can pay $19.95 to have it appear on the iOffer home page or $9.95 for a featured listing in the search results or category listings. If you have an idea of how much you'd like to receive for the item, you can set an asking price, but that's not necessary. You can also choose to simply entertain offers, as you might do if you placed a newspaper ad seeking the "best offer" for an item.

At this point, the power shifts to potential buyers. When someone stumbles upon an item that he or she wants, he or she can agree to pay the asking price or initiate negotiations by making an offer of his or her own. The seller can accept that offer or make a counteroffer until a fair price is reached. Sellers can negotiate simultaneously with multiple bidders and choose the best offer. (All negotiations are conducted in public on the "Questions and Offers" board that's part of each online listing.) IOffer listings last for 30 to 60 days, unless the seller accepts an offer before that time limit expires.

In addition to posting their own item advertisements, sellers have the option of trolling the "Wanted" classifieds at iOffer to see if they have an item that a buyer is searching for. Sellers can also sign up to receive "Buyer Alerts" via e-mail that notify them when someone posts a "Wanted" ad in a particular category. What's more, iOffer merchants may chime in on a negotiation between another seller and buyer, using the site's "Snag a Sale" feature. Essentially, sellers are allowed to eavesdrop on these negotiations and offer the buyer an identical item at a better price.

Whether you choose to run an online ad, find buyers through the "Wanted" ads, or "Snag a sale," you're obligated to pay iOffer a commission on every completed sale. The amount varies depending on the type of item you've sold and the final price. The site collects no fees for sales of aircraft, boats, cars, trucks, or real estate. On items priced up to $24.99, the fee ranges from 50 cents to $1.25. IOffer charges a 5 percent commission on sales worth $25 to $99.99. For items priced from $100 to $1,499.99, the site collects $5 plus 2.5 percent of the transaction amount over $100. For items worth $1,500 or more, the fee is $40, plus 1.5 percent of the transaction amount over $1,500.

Unlike most online marketplaces, iOffer prohibits its users from sharing information with one another until they enter into a transaction. That means that sellers cannot post any identifying information about themselves on their personal pages or in their iOffer ads. There can be no mention of personal or company names, no e-mail addresses, no street addresses, and no telephone numbers. Only after an offer has been made and accepted will iOffer provide the parties with one another's contact information. Presumably, this is done so that buyers and sellers don't cut iOffer out of its commissions by closing a deal off the site. This is certainly understandable, but it makes it diffi-cult for sellers wanting to maintain a single brand identity across multi-ple online marketplaces. If that's your goal, you may want to use iOffer only to market merchandise that you can't sell in other channels.

What Sells Best

Because iOffer touts haggling over bidding, the site is a perfect place to sell surplus inventory, namely those items that have been sitting on your virtual store shelves or that have failed to sell through the traditional online auction process. Luckily, iOffer makes it easy for sellers to import their dead stock from other marketplaces. All you have to do is run the Mr. Grabber or Web Grabber software and in-struct it to import your unsold items from eBay, Overstock, and other marketplaces. (Alternatively, you can use iOffer's bulk-listing tool at www.ioffer.com/sellerCenter.do?tab=BULK_UPLOAD to cre-ate a spreadsheet of all the items you want to list for sale.) You'll be given the option of setting asking prices and terms for each item.

Because there are no insertion fees and due to the longer dura-tion of the listings, iOffer is also a great place to sell inexpensive items. Consider it the perfect outlet for merchandise you wouldn't want to pay 35 cents to auction on eBay or even a few pennies to list in your eBay store. In fact, you may be able sell such items for no fee at the iOffer companion site iOfferLite, where all items are $4.99 or less. As with the main site, there are no listing fees. And the company routinely runs promotions where it charges no final-value fees on inexpensive items listed on iOfferLite.

In addition to these approaches, you may also find success listing products that iOffer designates as "Hot Items." At the time this book went to press, these included Microsoft Xbox 360 video game systems, tools, Christmas decor, collectible coins and money, designer clothing and accessories, cookbooks, and electronics. For an up-to-date list of "Hot Items," click on the "Buy" tab on the iOffer home page.

HALF.COM

The Lowdown

Unlike the other featured sites in this chapter, eBay subsidiary Half.com (at www.half.ebay.com) is a niche marketplace for selling books, textbooks, CDs, movies, video games, and video game systems at a fixed priced. In other words, it's not an auction site. Instead, it is positioned as a competitor to Amazon.com, although all inventory at Half.com is offered and shipped by third-party sellers.

Half.com makes its money not from listing fees, but rather through commissions on closed sales. Once posted, a listing on Half.com remains active until the item sells. It's therefore the best marketplace if you're looking to take a hands-off approach to selling. You can simply upload your inventory, then do nothing until orders start coming in. (However, you may find that you need to be more actively involved to improve your sell-through ratio. More on that later.)

Though its roots are with eBay, Half.com isn't nearly as popular as its bigger parent. Only about 1 percent of the millions of people who visit eBay click over to Half.com, according to Alexa, a web site traffic ranking service. Additionally, Half.com functions quite differently from the auction site. Indeed, shoppers are more likely to consider it an online store rather than an online marketplace because they're able to browse, click to fill up a shopping cart, and buy from multiple sellers using a secured credit card transaction processed by Half.com. When Half.com shoppers punch in the title of a book (*The eBay Millionaire*, for example), the search results return a listing of various sellers that have the title. The results are grouped by item condition—from brand-new to acceptable—and prices and feedback ratings for sellers are clearly displayed, allowing shoppers to make side-by-side comparisons. In addition, there are no variances in shipping charges among sellers, as is common on eBay. All shipping charges are set by Half.com and added to the sale price at checkout. The actual rate varies depending on the type of item being sold.

Half.com requires eBay sellers to register a separate account for billing purposes. But sellers can use the same user ID and password in both marketplaces, which makes cross-promotion of items possible. If you use the same seller ID on both Half.com and eBay, your feedback score will be aggregated and you'll be credited for transactions on both marketplaces. In addition, if you are selling more than one item on Half.com, customers visiting your Half.com shop will be able to click over to eBay to see what you're auctioning off and what you have for sale in your eBay store. Unfortunately, eBay doesn't provide reciprocal links to Half.com listings from its store or auction pages. So, if you want your eBay customers to know that you also sell on Half.com, you'll have to market to them directly with e-mail messages and package flyers.

Getting Started

Even if you have an active eBay account, you'll need to register again to sell on Half.com. Remember that you can choose the same user ID. This is certainly advisable because you'll start out with a high feedback score and your existing customers will be able to find you more easily. The main reason Half.com requires you to register a new account is to collect necessary financial data from you. You'll need to provide a valid credit card account and a telephone number for identity verification purposes. You'll also need to place your personal checking account information on file with Half.com, as you'll be paid twice monthly by direct deposit for any sales made on the site. Half.com deducts its commissions before paying you.

The next step is to begin listing books, movies, music, video games, and video game systems for sale. You can list items individually, but I don't recommend it, especially if you have a large inventory. Instead, follow the instructions on Half.com to create a file exchange spreadsheet that will allow you to post large quantities of merchandise in a single step. (Instructions are available online at http://pages.ebay.com/file_exchange/.) Some commercial software may also provide you with this capability.

One nice perk of selling on Half.com is that you don't have to provide your own photography or write your own descriptions. Like Amazon, the site maintains a catalog of millions of book, movie, CD, and video game titles. To make use of this powerful tool, all you have to do is provide the International Standard Book Number (ISBN) of any book you're selling and the Universal Product Code (UPC) for other merchandise. Once you type in the number, photographs and an item description automatically appear in your listing. It's very important to make sure the numbers you provide are accurate; otherwise you could end up posting an item that you don't really have in inventory. If you don't have the ISBN or UPC number—such as when you're selling a used item—you can use Half.com's search tool to find it. Just go to the site's home page and pretend you're a buyer searching for an item. Once you access an item from the search listings, you'll be offered the option to "Sell Yours Now!" When you click on that link, you'll be taken to another page that includes the ISBN or UPC number. If you're planning on bulk listing items, it's a good idea to begin by making a list of all these codes and numbers.

How It Works

Once you've taken care of the basics, you can move on to the more subjective parts of selling on Half.com. These are the decisions that will determine how much you sell on the site and how much money you make.

As in any online marketplace, Half.com shoppers want to know the condition of the item they're buying. On eBay, sellers accomplish this by posting photographs of the actual item and a detailed description of its features and flaws. On Half.com, you can't include your own pictures; you have to use the stock photography the site provides. In addition to the catalog description, sellers are able to write their own descriptive comments about an item. This is a great way to point out any unique features of your particular item. You could note, for example, that a book is autographed by the author or that a video game system comes with two free games. Perhaps your best way of describing an item is by accurately rating its condition—from brand-new to acceptable. Half.com requires that all items be rated in this way, but people have different ways of defining these terms. You'll do your customers—and yourself—a service by explaining what a particular rating means in your descriptive comments about the item. This ensures there are no surprises when a customer receives the item.

Half.com publishes guidelines for rating books and other items, and you can use those when scoring your items. Some booksellers, however, prefer to use collector's guidelines, which provide for more variances in condition—new, fine or like new, very good, good, fair/acceptable, and poor.

Price is another important factor when selling on Half.com. Most shoppers come to the site looking for deals and cheaper prices than they could find in stores or on other web sites. In fact, Half.com's selling point to consumers is that it's a place where they can "save every day" and find items at "drastically reduced prices." As a seller, your feedback on the site will help you win some business. But to make more customers click on and buy your items, you have to offer better pricing than your competitors.

When you post an item manually, Half.com will suggest a price, based on the item's condition and prevailing online retail prices. Half.com recommends that you list "like new" products at 50 percent off online retail, "very good" products at 45 percent of retail, "good" products at 40 percent of retail, and "acceptable" products at 35 percent of retail. This is a good rule of thumb, but you'll need to monitor your competitors' asking prices when determining what yours should be. Strive to be the low-price leader for every item you list at Half.com if you want to sell a lot of merchandise and turn over your inventory quickly.

Remember that Half.com sets shipping prices, so you won't be able to pad your profits with inflated shipping and handling charges. For example, buyers pay $2.78 for media mail shipping when buying a hardcover book and $2.40 when purchasing a paperback. You won't get any more money for shipping, even if it costs you more than that to package and mail the item. So, make sure to account for those expenses when setting your asking price. And don't forget to include Half.com's commissions in pricing calculations. Fees range from 7.5 percent of the total for items over $250 to 15 percent of the total for items priced $50 or less.

After you make a sale, Half.com will send you an e-mail with the buyer's order and shipping information. You have 72 hours (excluding holidays and weekends) to ship the product. Twice a month—on the 15th and the final day of the month—Half.com calculates what it owes you for completed transactions and initiates a direct deposit to your checking account. You should receive your money within seven business days of the transfer of the direct-deposit funds.

What Sells Best

What sells best on Half.com? Books, DVD and VHS movies, CDs, video games, and video game systems are the only items you can list here, but sellers must be choosy about which items they sell in these categories. On Half.com, you will be competing against both large and small sellers—meaning that some may have access to wholesale pricing. And you'll also be competing against merchants offering used merchandise. In many cases, consumers may not care if an item is new or used—only that the price is good. For those reasons, steer away from things like current best sellers and more ubiquitous items because it's virtually impossible to make money with these items on Half.com. Consider Dan Brown's novel, *The Da Vinci Code*, which was on best-seller lists for years and is available in both paperback and hardcover. Copies are available on Half.com for as little as 75 cents, and there's no profit to be made in that.

You'll do much better by specializing in items that are harder to find in retail outlets and online marketplaces. Depending on the item, demand could be quite high. Plus, you'll face decidedly less competition, enabling you to set a much higher (and more profitable) price for these items.

Because Half.com listings remain active until the item sells, you may also want to consider posting certain products for sale both here and in other marketplaces. For instance, you could list the same product at Half.com and at Amazon or eBay to tap into a wider customer base. Be careful in doing this, though. Either ensure that you have multiple quantities of the item or, if you're dealing with a unique item, be certain that your inventory management system can effectively handle these cross channels. If the item sells on Half.com, for example, you'll want the listing to be pulled from the other marketplaces immediately so you don't mistakenly sell the same item twice and encounter fulfillment problems.

Half.com Action Plan

Here's how to get your business up and running on Half.com:

- ✔ Register a user ID on Half.com. Be sure to use the same ID that you're using on eBay so existing customers will be able to find you. Your feedback score will transfer, as well. Half.com will link to your eBay auctions and eBay store items from your Half.com shop.

- ✔ Make sure that you have a record of all the ISBN and UPC numbers for the items you want to sell on Half.com. If not, use the search feature on the web site to identify these numbers and codes for each item.

- ✔ Grade the condition of each item you're selling using Half.com's guidelines and your own standards, which you should enumerate to your customers.

- ✔ Set your prices using Half.com's percentage-off retail guidelines, as well as your own inventory costs. Don't forget to account for additional shipping and handling costs when setting your prices. Check the marketplace to see how much other merchants are selling the same item for. Strive to have the lowest price.

✔ Create a spreadsheet that lists items you want to sell on Half.com. Upload your inventory to Half.com by following the instructions at http://pages.ebay.com/file_exchange/.

✔ Inform your existing customers via e-mail and through advertisements, mailings, and flyers that you're now selling on Half.com. Make sure they know your user ID and how to find your items.

✔ In addition to media mail and basic shipping, offer expedited methods to give your listings an edge over the competition.

✔ When a customer makes a purchase from you on Half.com, ship the item promptly using the promised method. Post feedback for buyers promptly and request that they do the same for you.

✔ Continuously monitor your unsold items on Half.com. If a competitor trumps your price, consider lowing your price if you can do so profitably.

✔ Transfer slow-selling merchandise from other marketplaces to Half.com, where listings remain active until the items sell.

PROS AND CONS OF THE VARIOUS AUCTION SITES

In this chapter, with the exception of Half.com, I've attempted to offer a sampling of the various types of online auction sites where sellers can hawk their wares beyond eBay. Believe me, there are dozens—Bid4Assets, Bidville, eBid, ePier, Wagglepop, OnlineAuction, PropertyRoom, Sell.com, whaBAM!, and OnSale, just to name a few. Some are clearly eBay imitators. But others attempt to differentiate themselves with distinctive features, alternative pricing strategies, and unique approaches to the buyer-seller relationships. A few target like-minded people. FaithBid, for example, is a site "connecting spirited buyers and sellers." There are even sites that tap into niche markets, such as iGavel (fine art, antiques, and collectibles), CigarBid (premium hand-rolled cigars), PGA Galleries (rare books, maps, and manuscripts), Audiogon (high-end audio equipment), and PenBid (fountain pens and antique pens).

As a seller, you can't possibly have a presence on every online auction site. Managing such an enterprise would tax even the most organized person and the most robust auction management software. But if you want your online business to grow, you *must* look beyond eBay for auction customers. True, eBay is the dominant auction marketplace and one of the world's busiest e-commerce sites. But it is becoming more crowded with each passing year, making it increasingly difficult for sellers to compete and capture buyers. And as fees continue to rise, many sellers are forced to look beyond eBay to maintain profitability.

Talk to smart online merchants, those who have successfully grown revenues and profits by branching out into different marketplaces, and you'll often hear them say, "I sell more items on eBay, but I make more money on other sites." That's the best argument I can make to convince you to give eBay's smaller competitors a try. Most of these sites are desperate to win business from the giant, so they're going to charge you less to sell there. You face fewer competitors, so you can set your asking prices higher—a factor that's likely to result in higher average selling prices. Armed with those realities, it's easy to do the math. Higher selling prices minus lower fees equals higher profits.

Of course, you can't expect these other auction sites to deliver the traffic or the customers that eBay does. It's unlikely that you'll ever reach the equivalent of Titanium PowerSeller status on a small auction site. The demand simply is not there—yet. But you may find that it's easier to build a multimillion-dollar business by selling on many sites versus one.

These are the facts. Even the executives at eBay's competitors don't dispute them. That said, you may find that some hot-selling items on eBay are real duds on other auction sites. Conversely, you may discover that certain items sell better on other sites than they ever do on eBay. It will take time to figure all this out.

In addition to being the biggest online auction site, eBay also has the advantage of having the strongest infrastructure. You won't find any auction management software that doesn't work with eBay. But some third-party programs won't integrate with smaller auction sites. In those cases, you'll have to determine whether it's still worth your while to sell in these marketplaces. If the answer is yes, you'll have the option of listing items for sale there manually, using that site's bulk-listing tool or choosing a different auction management provider that works with more sites. This may prove to be a bigger barrier than you think. Manually managing auctions in multiple marketplaces is time-consuming, and it also increases the chance of errors. Imagine what might happen to your business if you accidentally list the same item on two marketplaces and sell it on both marketplaces. That's the kind of fulfillment issue that could erode your reputation with customers and even put you out of business.

Weigh the pros and cons carefully and evaluate them for each individual auction site before embarking on your own multichannel strategy.

Action Plan

To get your business up and running on the various alternative auction sites, do the following:

- ✔ Evaluate your profitability on eBay. Subtract all your costs (including insertion, listing, PayPal, final-value, and other fees) from your revenues to determine exactly how much money you're making with your eBay business.
- ✔ Investigate other online auction sites to determine where else you might sell your products.
- ✔ Find out if your auction management software supports selling on these other sites.

✔ Register with a few of the most attractive sites for your business and begin familiarizing yourself with the buying and selling process, as well as the fee structure.

✔ Begin listing inexpensive items for sale on these other sites to see how bidders respond to you and your items.

✔ Be sure to make your listings look as professional as possible. Use branded templates so bidders recognize you as a reputable business. If the other sites allow it, promote your own web site in every auction listing and reference your reputation and experience on eBay.

✔ Alert your existing customers (through e-mail, mailings, announcements on your web site, shipping flyers, and other means) that you're now offering products on sites other than eBay.

✔ Offer bidders incentives, like free shipping or free gifts, if they buy from you on these other sites.

✔ Continue selling (and buying) in these other marketplaces to build up a respectable feedback score or rating.

After each quarter, evaluate your performance, revenues, and profits on each online auction site, including eBay. Have your sales increased as a result of the change? Are profits higher? Are costs lower?

Alternative Auction Site Success Story

GEMaffair

For a while, Michael Jansma was riding high on eBay's popularity and momentum. The online jewelry merchant was raking in about a half million dollars' worth of sales every month through his eBay store and auctions.

Then, about two and a half years ago, he noticed his revenue starting to decline. His business was hurt further by eBay fee hikes, which tightened the squeeze on his profit margin. Unwilling to let competition and higher operating expenses defeat his entrepreneurial spirit, Jansma quickly sought to diversify and began marketing jewelry heavily on his own web site, plus Overstock, Amazon, and Property-Room.com, as well as on eBay.

Jansma, the proprietor of GEMaffair, which is based in Largo, Florida, discovered the Internet as a marketplace in 1996 after making money selling Beanie Babies on eBay. Jansma had owned a bricks-and-mortar jewelry store in Florida since 1994. After his success with the Beanie Babies, he began dabbling in selling jewelry online, listing some items for sale on his own web site and others in online auctions on eBay. To say the business took off is an understatement. Within just a few years, Jansma was pulling in millions of dollars on eBay, mostly through jewelry auctions that began with 99-cent starting bids. By 2000, nearly all of Jansma's eggs were in one basket, with eBay accounting for 99 percent of revenues.

But after a few years Jansma began to slowly back away from eBay and shifted more of his sales to other online marketplaces. Now, eBay accounts for just 55 percent of GEMaffair's business, which totals in the millions of dollars annually. While Jansma won't provide specific figures, GEMaffair sells thousands of jewelry items every month, with monthly sales totaling in the six-figure range. Jansma projects revenues will reach $750,000 every month—or $9 million annually—within the next two to three years and that his company's net income will increase as operations become more streamlined and efficient.

"EBay is a great source of cash flow, and you want to retain those customers," he says. "But you can only grow so much with competition and declining markets. It's the most efficient marketplace, but it's also the lowest-margin marketplace."

Since scaling back his eBay presence, Jansma has focused his efforts on building the GEMaffair brand, specifically by being in every marketplace where his customers might go looking for jewelry. "With the brand we're building, we're going after the everyday shopper," he explains. "We're looking to gain a percentage of the business that's already there. The jewelry that we sell is stuff that you're going to buy to go along with a specific outfit. You're going to spend $50 to $100 on jewelry to match a specific outfit."

Jansma owns some 80 to 100 Internet domain names, many of which link directly to his company's main web site, www.gemaffair.com. Among the sites he owns: www.diamondrubyrings.com, www.discount gemstonering.com, along with www.birthstonesforjanuary.com, www .birthstonesforfebruary.com, and all 10 other months. The idea, Jansma says, is to capture shoppers who use the search engines to find a particular type of jewelry. In his search-engine optimization, Jansma uses very specific descriptive keywords, the same phrases that shoppers would use to find a specific type or piece of jewelry. "We've purchased keyword phrases," he says. "We believe that people are going to type in 'birthstones for March.'"

Another way Jansma drives traffic to his site is by positioning it as more than just a shopping destination. "We actually invest a lot of time and energy in educating customers," he notes. "We have found that they remember and appreciate that." In addition to product listings, the site includes an "Educate Yourself" section where consumers can learn about diamond grading, colored gemstones, jewelry care, and the difference between karats and carats. There are also ring-sizing tips, a ring-sizing chart with European conversions, and a glossary of terms commonly used in the jewelry industry. Such features help boost GEMaffair's search engine rankings, and they also attract a host of potential buyers. "Anything we can do to keep our name in the forefront of our customers is beneficial to us," Jansma maintains. What's more, he says, it's good customer service. "I just don't see any detriment to providing this information."

Across every marketplace, GEMaffair works hard to reflect a consistent brand to its customers. Customers see identical photography, logos, and product information, whether they're looking at an item for sale on eBay, Amazon, Overstock, PropertyRoom, or the company's own web site. However, items are priced to the specific marketplace.

Factors such as traffic, fees, and customer expectations all play a role in Jansma's pricing decisions.

In the earlier days of his business, Jansma advocated a pricing strategy that is still favored by many high-volume eBay sellers. He priced nearly every auction at 99 cents and allowed bidders to duke it out over the final price. Before eBay was overrun by competition, before dozens—if not hundreds—of like items began appearing on the site, that was a lucrative way to do business. Most items ended up selling for a tidy profit. Now Jansma finds it difficult to profit with the 99-cent starting bid model, and he's more likely to list items for sale on eBay at a fixed price or with a starting bid much closer to the actual market price. (Of course, there are a few exceptions. Around Mother's Day, he lists mom-themed jewelry items for 99 cents and counts on strong consumer demand to drive up the price.)

On other auction sites, like Overstock or PropertyRoom, he typically sets the opening bid higher than he would on eBay, specifically to account for the lower traffic and to better serve customers who choose those sites over eBay.

"Generally, people on Overstock are fed up with eBay," he says. "They are not looking to hunt as much, so they go to Overstock.com or Overstock Auctions. I think they're willing to pay a little bit more with a little less risk.

"I think there's a ton on traffic on Overstock and it's converting to sales," Jansma adds. "This is not the kind of shopper who wants to play around and bid and watch and bid and watch. Our average selling price on Overstock is higher than on eBay, but we don't sell as many items."

Likewise, GEMaffair's average selling price for identical items is higher on Amazon.com than on eBay to account for the higher transaction fees and different customer service expectations. "On Amazon, I'm charged three times the commission I'm charged on eBay," Jansma says. "On Amazon, I'm required to provide a 30-day return policy. EBay lets me set my own terms and conditions," he says. "It's a lot more expensive to do business on Amazon than on eBay. On Amazon, you have to take a credit card. Amazon requires you to ship in a certain number of days. But our average selling price on Amazon over eBay is higher.

"The bottom line is, we get more from Amazon," Jansma concludes. "Amazon handles all payment procurement and all of the risk and most of the contact with the customer. So, that's pretty beneficial."

Though there is considerable crossover, Jansma believes that each online marketplace has its own unique customer base. He tries to cater directly to their preferences. EBay shoppers, for example, enjoy hunting for a bargain and besting other consumers in a bidding war. Hence, he sets auction prices lower on eBay. Overstock Auctions shoppers don't like the hunt nearly as much, and they aren't as concerned with scoring a bargain. They want to easily find a product and bid on it, without fear of fraud and without worrying that someone will snap it up at the last minute. That explains why GEMaffair products are priced higher on Overstock. A customer who shops through a search engine most likely is searching for a very specific item, and that's why Jansma is diligent about including specific keywords in every product listed on his web site.

Comparison-shopping traffic heats up around the holidays because people have run out of time to shop, blown through their budgets, or can't find a product locally. In response, Jansma sends product feeds to the comparison-shopping engines only during the final quarter of the year when clicks are more likely to convert to sales. Amazon customers are accustomed to shopping online and expect a certain level of service, like flexible return policies, quick shipping, the ability to pay by credit card, and even nicer gift boxes. Again, Jansma does what he can to oblige those preferences.

Internally, GEMaffair has benchmarks that it must meet to ensure that every sale is profitable. Jansma won't disclose his target profit margin, but he does explain how he arrives at that figure for every item.

In his business, the most costly part of selling an item is creation of the product ad, which includes photography and a detailed description of the item. "The majority of our success is due to the time we invest in our ads," he says. For those reasons, Jansma buys only items that he can purchase in bulk and stays away from products that are just available in small quantities. Once an ad is created, it can easily be posted on multiple marketplaces.

When Jansma brings a new product into inventory, he sets a lower profit-margin expectation for the first batch he sells to account for the time and effort spent preparing the ad. But when he restocks the item, he aims for a higher profit margin because the expensive up-front work has already been done. If a product consistently fails to deliver on those expectations, he may remove it from inventory and replace it with a more lucrative piece of jewelry.

"I leave the rarer things and one-of-a-kind type of items for other people," Jansma, whose inventory includes between 1,700 and 2,200 active SKUs, explains. "There are plenty of people out there who sell jewelry in my category who want to buy one, two, or three of an item."

Jansma uses software from Infopia to automate and manage his multichannel online business. He investigated about 40 other auction management solutions, including the popular ChannelAdvisor product, before settling on Infopia. For him, the primary appeal was that he could customize Infopia to fit his own business. Another bonus was the fact that he wouldn't have to pay Infopia a commission on every sale. His investment in the software has been a costly, but necessary, expense. Jansma estimates that he has spent at least a six-figure amount on custom-development fees with Infopia and other programmers. That total doesn't include the monthly subscription fee he pays to Infopia. But the up-front investment has been worthwhile and helped ease GEMaffair's transition from eBay PowerSeller to multi-channel online business.

Jansma manages all his online sales from within Infopia, regardless of the marketplace. In fact, Infopia even hosts his the GEMaffair web site. When it's time to list an item for sale, Jansma can easily post it in multiple marketplaces with just a few keystrokes. "We literally go into Infopia, check a specific box, and can select from multiple choices where to put that ad, picture, or set of attributes," he says.

GEMaffair is proof positive that eBay isn't the only path to online success. Company proprietor Michael Jansma remains a top-level PowerSeller on eBay. Yet he has also been able to sustain revenues and increase profits while migrating more and more of his business to other smaller online marketplaces. And, in just a few years, he's poised to bring in more sales than he ever did on eBay, thanks to a marketing strategy that includes aggressive search-engine optimization, a stand-alone web site, and such sites as Overstock, Amazon, and Property-Room along with the various comparison-shopping engines.

Alternative Auction Site Success Story

Pennyworth Sales

When companies are going through tumultuous times, they often call Dale and Judy Oglesby of Pennyworth Sales. For 26 years, their business has been liquidating unwanted or damaged merchandise for other companies. In times of fires, hurricanes, bankruptcies, and mergers, the Oglesbys show up to purchase leftover inventory.

For much of their company's history, the Oglesbys sold this excess inventory through their retail store in Columbus, Kansas, a tiny town of about 3,500 near the Kansas-Missouri state line. Columbus nurtured the Oglesbys' small-town sensibilities, and it was a nice place to raise a family and get to know your neighbors. But the small population and mining-based economy haven't always made it easy to run a business. For most of their company's history, the Oglesbys have been locked into buying only excess inventory they could sell locally or through Dale's industrial contacts.

But that all changed in 2001 when eToys, another casualty of the dot-com bust, filed for Chapter 11 bankruptcy and quickly went out of business. Pennyworth Sales handled liquidation of two of the company's distribution centers in Ontario and Commerce, California. The Oglesbys brought 17 tractor-trailer loads of merchandise to Columbus. Each truck was filled with enough toys, games, dolls, and stuffed animals to overwhelm even the greediest child. The inventory was massive and varied—everything from affordable toy trucks to expensive collector's dolls. The Oglesbys knew from experience that there were probably too many toys to sell through their local retail store. At some point, local demand would surely dry up, and they'd have to start slashing prices like crazy to turn the inventory. Even so, the eToys inventory was too rich a bounty to pass up.

Luckily, the Oglesbys' daughter happened to be working at her parents' warehouse when they began sorting through the truckloads of toys. When she spotted a stash of Madame Alexander dolls, she nagged her parents to put them online, specifically on eBay. Just because eToys had gone belly-up trying to sell toys online didn't mean that the Internet wasn't a viable marketplace, she reasoned. The Oglesbys capitulated to their daughter's wishes and listed the dolls for sale on eBay. Every single one sold—for a profit. "I was surprised that they sold at all," Judy admits. "I had no idea that eBay was that broad a market."

By February 2002, Pennyworth Sales was officially in business online. Judy used eBay as a secondary liquidation channel for the business. She'd put specialty items (like the collector dolls) up for bid, and she'd also auction off items that had been sitting on store shelves for a while. "We used eBay to get rid of the tail ends of stock," she explains. Within a month, the online side of the business grew to where Judy had to hire her best friend to help manage it. Four years later, Pennyworth Sales employs eight people, in addition to the Oglesbys. Six of these workers concentrate their efforts on the Internet side of the business. Judy estimates she could stand to have five additional computers and employees to help manage auctions on eBay and Overstock, plus the for-sale listings on the company's own web site at www.pennyworthsales.com. Internet sales, which were once a quarter of the company's sales, now total about half of Pennyworth Sales' annual revenues.

The fact that Pennyworth Sales is still in business is perhaps even more striking than those Internet-driven financial statistics. Dale Oglesby, who has always been the buyer and backbone of the company, was stricken with a debilitating disease in 2003 that kept him out of work for six months and nearly killed him. Doctors eventually diagnosed that he was suffering from the Epstein-Barr virus, a form of mononucleosis that is characterized by a persistent fever and sore throat, swollen lymph nodes, fatigue, and malaise, and can progress to more life-threatening symptoms. While Dale battled the disease, his wife struggled to care for him and keep their business afloat. It's only because they were selling online and reaching a much broader customer base than their local market that they were able to keep Pennyworth Sales in business during that period when no new inventory was coming in. "The Internet saved our bacon," Judy says. "If I hadn't been on the Internet during that time, we would have gone broke."

Credit patience, smart inventory procurement and management, strong customer service, auction management software, and an emphasis on repeat business for Pennyworth Sales' growth and success online.

Operating in several online channels, as well as a bricks-and-mortar store, the Oglesbys have to choose the best venue for each product they sell. Judy, who manages the company's Internet operations while her husband focuses on procurement, has one hard-and-fast rule of thumb when it comes to selling online. She markets only brand-new products on the web site, eBay, and Overstock. Anything that is being liquidated because of its condition (say because of smoke damage in a fire) automatically goes into the bricks-and-mortar store inventory. As for brand-new items, Oglesby chooses the best marketplace based on previous experience and her own gut instinct. For example, practical items such as tools and household goods sell best on eBay. Those are the kinds of items that the Oglesbys would have avoided buying altogether just a few years ago because they knew there wouldn't be enough local demand for the products. But the Internet has opened up new markets for them, by offering exposure to a worldwide customer base. "We sell kitchen utensils like pastry brushes and poultry lacers to places like Sitka, Alaska," Judy says. "We ship everyday kitchen goods to Wyoming and Montana." If there's one lesson Judy has learned online, it's this: Just because an item seems commonplace doesn't mean it is. What's a dime a dozen in your town may be a needle in a haystack one state over.

While eBay shoppers clamor for everyday goods at bargain prices, the same can't be said for those consumers who browse and buy on Overstock, Judy says. Instead, jewelry and collectibles do well and command higher prices on the hybrid auction-outlet site, she says. And those customers who come directly to the Pennyworth Sales web site are typically familiar with the company's products and looking for something specific, like a drill bit, or else they're hunting for a bargain. Therefore, Pennyworth Sales uses its own web site for promoting things like tools, building supplies, and inexpensive gifts. The web site also features a sampling of what the company has for sale in its online auctions and eBay store.

Oftentimes, depending on the product, Judy may market identical items on Overstock, on eBay, and in the bricks-and-mortar store to determine which can deliver the biggest profit. She also scouts the various sites, looking for niches that Pennyworth Sales can fill. For example, when she began selling on Overstock, Judy spent eight weeks familiarizing herself with the site and browsing through all the categories to see what other merchants were selling. She wisely has focused on those categories with the least competition and the fewest number of items for sale. "That way I know that my products will be seen," she says. She follows a similar tack on eBay, often choosing to list, not in the hot categories, but rather in less crowded marketplaces where her items are sure to show up at the top of shoppers' search results.

When she decided to sell on Overstock, Judy registered the same user ID, bluepennylady, that she had been using on eBay, so existing customers could easily find her. And she took things one step further by sending out an e-mail blast alerting all of her previous Internet customers that she was now selling on Overstock, as well as eBay. Finally, she carefully watched the behavior of the eBay bidders. She noticed that sometimes eBay shoppers would put her auctions on their watch lists and then fail to bid. Many watchers would contact her after an auction's end and ask to purchase the item directly. Rather than doing this, she would relist the item on Overstock Auctions and direct shoppers there. Her retail customers also got what Judy calls "sack stuffers," flyers alerting them to new inventory that would be going on the auction block at Overstock. It was through these techniques that Judy was able to drive her own traffic to Overstock and build up her seller rating, which helped her attract even more bidders. In the beginning, when her seller rating was low, Judy was also careful to list mostly inexpensive items on Overstock. Most shoppers wouldn't hesitate to buy an inexpensive item from a low-ranked seller, she reasoned, but they might be skeptical about buying a high-priced item from a new seller. "I figured out that if I was going to get good money, I needed to get good feedback," she said. "Now on Overstock, some of my higher-priced items are beginning to sell because now I've got a higher rating."

Judy also uses the online marketplaces to sell items that have been sitting on her store shelves for too long. Rather than marking something down so much that she's almost giving it away, Judy will attempt to sell it online, either through an auction or in her eBay store. Typically, if something is valued at just a few dollars, it goes directly into her eBay store where listing fees are much lower than the 35-cent base rate for an auction. Things get a bit trickier for items valued around $9. Typically, Judy will run a few test auctions to determine the market price for the item. If it continually sells for more than $9.99, she'll keep selling it through the auction format. But if it sells for less than that, she'll put it in the eBay store to minimize her listing expenses.

Another strategy Judy employs: using low-priced auctions to tease shoppers to visit her eBay store or other auctions. In the liquidation business, the Oglesbys often buy huge quantities of the same item and move them through the various channels. When faced with a large quantity, Judy often will simultaneously post an item for auction and in her eBay store. The idea, she says, is to pique interest in the product with her auction in the hope of driving Buy It Now buyers to her store. Listing an item for sale in both formats ensures that it shows up in search listings. (Remember that eBay store listings don't always show up in main search results; it depends on how crowded the category is.)

Overstock Auctions does not yet allow merchants to operate their own stores on its site. But Oglesby employs a similar strategy to draw attention to and increase interest in her auctions. She'll often auction a mid-priced item for much less than it's really worth, employing the same loss-leader strategy that many bricks-and-mortar retailers use to attract customers to their stores. "If I sell a pair of earrings for 99 cents and this buyer likes me, she will buy from me again and tell her mom, her grandma, and so forth," Judy says.

Unlike many online auctioneers, Pennyworth Sales has an enviable record of repeat business. Two years ago, the company was ranked in the top 10 for repeat business on eBay. Even now, the company's repeat-buyer rate on eBay is 82 percent. On Overstock, the company has a 75 percent repeat-buyer rate. How has Pennyworth Sales been able to accomplish this? Oglesby chalks it up to superior customer service—the kind of thing you'd expect from a small-town retailer. But savvy marketing also has played a role.

Pennyworth Sales maintains a database of its past Internet sales, which enables the company to target market to past customers. Judy uses an inexpensive program to record the e-mail addresses of everyone who has purchased from Pennyworth Sales in the past. Every month, she notifies those customers by e-mailabout new merchandise for sale online.

In addition, when customers contact the company after a sale, customer service agents are able to pull up their order history. This functionality gives customers the illusion that the agent remembers them. "I get the feedback that our people are friendly, prompt, honest, and personal," Judy says. A customer recently e-mailed Judy asking if she had any more of an item that he'd purchased two years ago. Judy checked her auction and inventory management system to determine exactly what the man had ordered. Unfortunately, she had long ago sold out of the specific item he wanted. But she was able to offer him an acceptable alternative, and he placed another order.

Judy Oglesby has been so successful as an Internet merchant that she now teaches other retailers in her community how to succeed online. Her tips alone could fill a book. But there are a few key points she makes whenever she's instructing would-be online entrepreneurs:

- *Auction management software is crucial.* Judy, who used to audit software, uses Auction Wizard 2000. You load the software directly onto your computer rather than accessing it through the Web, as is the case with so many other auction management programs. Judy considers this a key selling point of Auction Wizard 2000 because she doesn't have to worry about security as she would with a Web-based application. The program costs $75 in the first year and $50 for tech support annually thereafter. "That's dog cheap," Judy says. (Web hosting through www.pair.com costs the company an additional $5.95 a month.)

- *"Thank you" goes a long way.* Every customer who purchases from Pennyworth Sales receives a thank-you with their shipment. The printed note includes the company's Web address, as well as its Overstock and eBay auction IDs.

- *Use shipping calculators.* After integrating shipping calculators into her online auctions, Judy saw an immediate 25 percent increase in her sell-through rate. In the long term, her sell-through rate has increased by nearly 50 percent now that bidders can get an accurate estimate of delivery charges.

- *Don't gouge customers, but never underestimate costs either.* Initially, Pennyworth Sales did not include the cost of packing materials in its shipping charge to consumers. But those expenses were cutting into profit margins, and the company now charges a $1 packing fee for anything shipped via the U.S. Postal Service and $2 for anything delivered by UPS.

- *Be prepared to lose money—sometimes.* Within any business, profit margins on individual items vary. It's no different with online selling. Some products will deliver huge profits, but others will cost you money to sell. Don't fret over *occasional* losses. "The bottom line is you're going to lose money on some stuff no matter how hard you try," Judy says. "But you'll make up the difference on something else."

- *Don't expect to make a profit right away.* Though Judy was lucky enough to profit from her first Internet sales of those Madame Alexander dolls, that's not the experience of many upstart sellers. It takes time to learn how the different online marketplaces work and to understand the bidding and pricing nuances of each one. You may need to aggressively market your auctions (either to existing customers or by using tools available online) before you start receiving bids. "When you go online, make up your mind that you may not make a dime for the first six weeks," Judy advises. "List things online that you really don't care how much money they bring. And then treat those customers as if they have spent $10,000 with you. If you do that, they will return."

6

Search-Engine Marketing

As an online entrepreneur, you are probably aware that there are two types of results displayed whenever you type a query into a search engine: *natural* (sometimes called organic) results and *paid* results. Both are extremely relevant to your success as an online retailer.

For an illustration of how online search works, type a simple phrase, such as "running shoes," into each of the three major search engines—Google, Yahoo!, and MSN Search. Depending on the site, you'll notice that some results are displayed on a blue background near the top of the page, while others show up under the heading "Sponsor Results," "Sponsored Links," or "Sponsored Sites." These sponsor results represent *paid* placements, and the featured web sites have outbid their competitors for the privilege of being listed in these prominent locations. If you click on one of these sponsored links, that advertiser will have to pay the search engine for driving your business to the site.

The other web sites listed in the search results are ranked based on their relevancy to the search term "running shoes." These are the *natural* search results. A site's ranking here is based on a variety of factors, including how many times the keyword "running shoes" appears within the site's content, how many other web sites link to the page, how many times the search term appears within the hidden source code on the web site, and a variety of other complicated and proprietary measures used by the search engines.

From your standpoint as an online merchant, it's important that your site ranks high in both natural and paid search so potential customers can easily find and buy from you. Your own budget, the competitive arena, and shopper habits will all play a role in how much energy and resources you devote to improving your rankings in each category. Generally, *search-engine optimization* is the term used to describe a web site's efforts to rank higher in natural or organic search, while search-engine marketing refers to paid campaigns. However, some people use the terms interchangeably, so I'll make sure to be clear as I discuss the two strategies going forward.

As a merchant, there are three main search engines that you need to concern yourself with because they account for more than three-quarters of all Internet search traffic. Not surprisingly, given that its name has become synonymous with search, Google is the most popular, with just under 50 percent of search traffic. Google is followed by Yahoo!, which handles about one-quarter of all Internet searches, and MSN Search, which processes about 12 percent of searches, according to Nielsen//NetRatings statistics.

Whether you're implementing a natural or paid search campaign, your goal should be for your web site to appear "above the fold" (that is, in the top half of the screen), because consumers are most likely to click on those links. On each major search engine, there's a limited amount of space above the fold; some is allocated for paid search results and the remainder displays organic results. On Yahoo!, just 16 percent of available clicks above the fold are reserved for natural search—which means that if you want to show up on the first screen there, you'll probably have to pay to do so. On Google and MSN Search, about one-third of the space on the first screen of search pages is reserved for natural search results, so you may not find it necessary to spend as much to capture clicks on these sites.

However, the game is not over once a searcher clicks on a link. Your ultimate objective is to turn searches into clicks and clicks into purchases. Your campaigns, therefore, should deliver relevant and motivated customers. The best way to accomplish this is by focusing your search-engine optimization and marketing on the best possible keywords—those that are relevant to what you sell and match what buyers already are searching for on the Web. You'll learn specific strategies for how to do this in the following sections of this book.

Getting Started

Before you can start optimizing your web site to improve your rankings in the search engines, you'll first need to make sure that Google, Yahoo!, MSN Search, and the other search engines even know your site exists. The first step is to have your site indexed in these various search engines and other widely referenced online directories like the Open Directory Project. You may have to pay a fee to index a commercial web site, but this will be well worth the money because it will bring paying customers to your site.

"If your site isn't indexed, you're not getting traffic," says Kevin McCarthy, vice president of search services for ChannelAdvisor.

Luckily, indexing your site is a relatively easy process, although you may discover that you'll need to manually submit your site to the various search engines to ensure you're recognized. (On the Yahoo! Home page, follow the link for "How to Suggest a Site" to begin the indexing process. You can also go directly to the indexing page at http://search.yahoo.com/info/submit.html. For Google, visit www .google.com/addurl/?continue=/addurl. And to be indexed with MSN Search, visit http://search.msn.com/docs/submit.aspx). You can register directly with the smaller search engines as well. If you can't find a link on the engine's home page, do a quick help search on the terms "add URL" or "index my site" for site-specific instructions. During the indexing process, many of the search engines will give you the opportunity to add comments about your site. By all means, do this, using keywords that accurately describe its content. It is important to include the keywords and specific search terms that customers are likely to use to find your site. This is not the place for marketing language, according to Search Engine Watch, an online news site that covers the search engine industry.

In addition to registering with the big three search engines, it's also a good idea to submit your web site to the Open Directory Project, the most comprehensive human-edited directory on the Web. It aims to be the most definitive catalog of the Internet, and you will benefit from submitting your site here because afterward it will be indexed with AOL Search, Google, Netscape Search, Yahoo!, and hundreds of other sites. To become listed in the Open Directory, visit the project's home page at www.dmoz.org and click on the "Add URL" link. You may also visit the page directly at http://dmoz.org/add.html. If your site is accepted into the Open Directory, it may take anywhere from two weeks to several months for it to be listed on the various partner sites that use Open Directory data. So, don't neglect to index your site with the major search engines immediately, or your traffic may suffer.

For step-by-step instructions on indexing your site, including how to make sure it is indexed quickly, you may want to check out Search Engine Watch's online guide, "Essentials of Search Engine Submission," at http://searchenginewatch.com/webmasters/index.php #essentials.

Indexing your site will ensure that you're included in natural search rankings, but it won't necessarily gain you high results. In fact, it probably won't. You'll need to do a bit more work to raise your profile with the search engines and trump your competitors. One of the easiest things you can do is make sure that other sites on the Web are linking to yours. In fact, the more links you have, the better because this will improve your standings in the search engine rankings. To determine your site's link popularity, you should install the Google toolbar, available for free download at http://toolbar.google.com. By clicking on the Page Info icon on the toolbar, you can view all the backwards links that are pointing to your web site (or any other site, for that matter.) For example, about 751,000 individual web sites link to eBay—pretty impressive.

If your backwards links number could use some boosting, ask your family members, friends, vendors, suppliers, and even your customers to link to you from their web sites. If you operate multiple sites, make sure to link to yourself. You may also be able to solicit some links at industry-specific portals or through trade groups of which you're a member. EBay and Overstock both have professional sellers' organizations, and its members often help to promote one another's sites. There are even companies that specialize in hooking up web site owners so they can provide reciprocal links to each other's sites. And there's no reason that you can't establish your own reciprocal links program, as Brad Fallon and his wife Jennifer did at their top-rated site, MyWeddingFavors.com.

Aside from links, content also factors heavily into natural search rankings. Simply put, you want to reference those terms that your customers are typing into the search engines on your site as many times as possible. Certainly, many people will search for generic terms, like "running shoes," "digital cameras," or "baby furniture." But you'll need to be much more detailed and specific than that if you want to convert search results into sales.

Fortunately, Web tools like Wordtracker (www.wordtracker.com) and the Yahoo! Keyword Selector Tool (http://searchmarketing.yahoo .com/rc/srch/) can help you home in on the most popular searches for your product category, based on actual Web searches on the topic conducted during the previous month.

Let's use the example of "baby furniture." In addition to the more than 53,000 searches conducted for that broad term, people also searched for "discount baby furniture" (2,241 searches), "baby dream furniture" (2,237 searches), "baby nursery furniture" (1,470 searches), "baby furniture store" (1,230 searches) and "used baby furniture" (1,073 searches). People also searched frequently for the term "baby furniture" in combination with specific brand names, such as Simmons, Pali, Simplicity, Graco, Da Vinci, and Storkcraft. While the volume is lower for these more specific search terms, you're more likely to find motivated buyers and up your conversion rate when you use them in your search-engine optimization strategy. In general, ChannelAdvisor's Kevin McCarthy says, branded terms convert best, followed by product terms, and then category terms.

Now, here's how to put these lessons to use on your web site: When designing your web pages and product listings, you'll have many opportunities to insert keywords into the text as well as into the hidden web site coding that is visible only to the search engines. Make sure to include specific product terms (and brands, where applicable) in the title, category, and description fields within your site to increase your search relevance. When creating product headlines, come up with a standard format. A good rule of thumb is to list the product brand name first, followed by the model name or number, any special characteristics or features, and finally the category. For example: "Canon DC100 5 megapixel digital camera" or "Kate Spade Amanda multicolor size 8 wedge shoes." To further optimize your site, you'll also want to include meta tags—coding that is invisible to visitors but that provides important information to the search engines about what your web site is about.

By including as many keywords as possible, you'll help to ensure that your site ranks high and stands out to searchers. In search results, every time a search term matches a keyword on your web site, that term will appear in bold, making your site stand out that much more from your competitors' sites.

In conjunction with your search-engine optimization efforts, you'll probably want to invest in a paid search campaign for your web site. Essentially, you will be advertising your site and products with the search engines. Again, the keywords you choose will determine your success. Your two best options are to begin with Google AdWords and Yahoo! Sponsored Search, each of which also gives you the opportunity to purchase exposure on other web sites and marketplaces.

The first step to creating a successful search advertising campaign is once again to identify a list of keywords and phrases that your customers are likely to use to find your products and business. Once you've determined those keywords, write a search listing for each one—including a title and description about your site. This is the information Web surfers will see when they search on your keywords, and you should take time writing these descriptions. After all, they are ads for your business, as important as a roadside billboard or a television commercial.

You'll be given the opportunity to bid on these keywords in order to ensure that when someone searches for a given term, your site shows up near the top of the sponsored search results. Results are ranked based on your bid amount. You may have to bid a lot for a broad or generic term if you want to figure prominently in the search results. However, the good news is that you'll pay these charges only when someone clicks on your sponsored search result. Your cost per click could be anywhere from a few pennies to as much as $100, depending on the keyword and the number of advertisers competing for top placement.

In general, you want to bid enough so that your site shows up within the top three paid listings on the search results page, as those are the most likely to generate clicks and conversions. When you embark on a search-engine advertising campaign, you'll also want to bid on a variety of keywords—both broad and specific—to maximize your results.

At Yahoo!, you can even see what your competitors are willing to pay per click for each keyword using the site's Keyword Selector or View Bids tools. This will help you set your maximum bid accordingly. Unfortunately, Google doesn't reveal this type of information to its AdWords customers, so you'll have to rely on the site's recommendations and its Traffic Estimator to determine exactly how much to bid on any specific keyword.

If not managed properly, a pay-per-click advertising campaign can quickly grow out of hand and become too expensive to manage. Fortunately, you can control your pay-per-click advertising costs by setting a daily budget of how much you're willing to spend on any particular keyword. Once your clicks total that amount, your ad will be pulled from the search rankings until the next day.

How It Works

The aim of any type of search-engine marketing, whether natural or paid, is to generate sales. You want people to click through to your web site from the search engines and buy your products once they're on your site. The ideal is to generate the most converted clicks for the lowest amount of money, by employing a combination of natural search-optimization techniques and bidding on a number of low-cost, low-volume, high-converting search terms.

As indicated, your optimization and marketing campaigns will be only as good as your keywords. But how do you find the best ones? I've already covered some strategies, such as using the keyword selection tools. But if you have experience selling on the Web, you probably have the answers at your fingertips. You just may not know how to find them. First, methodically analyze the content of your web site (or online auctions) and note any specific and general terms that could become keywords. These would include frequently mentioned categories of products, types of products, or brand names. By combining these terms with value-based modifiers that searchers may use to find these products—words like "discount," "unique," "new," "low-price," "specialty," and the like—you're likely to come up with a long list of specific keywords that have the potential to drive sales. You can also take a more analytical approach and examine the behavior of your existing customers. For example, using the various analytical tools on eBay, you can determine what searches bidders are using to find your products and items like them. Be sure to examine data within your Web log to see the actual search terms people used to find your web site. And if you have an internal search function on your web site, monitor search patterns to see what items people are shopping for inside your e-commerce store. This will help you identify good keywords to use in your paid and natural campaigns.

I've been throwing around the term "keywords" pretty freely in this chapter. In the context of search marketing, a keyword doesn't have to be a single word. In fact, the best keywords, in terms of search rankings and conversion rates, include multiple words—usually nouns and various modifiers. The majority of active keywords are two to three words long, according to statistics from DoubleClick and Performics, and four-word terms account for 12 percent of all active keywords.

Interestingly, an analysis by Oneupweb, a search-engine optimization and marketing firm, discovered that longer strings of keywords result in higher conversion rates (or more sales), peaking at four-word keyword phrases. In the study, conversion rates for four-word phrases were as high as 38 percent, meaning that more than one-third of people who clicked on a company's search link completed a purchase. The conversion rate was as high as 33 percent for three-word phrases, and as high as 15 percent for two-word phrases, according to the study.

There was one notable exception to the theory that longer keyword phrases result in higher conversions: single-word keywords comprised of corporate names have very high conversion rates. Examples of one-word branded keywords include Mustang, Pampers, Dustbuster, Maytag—basically names that are synonymous with a particular product. However, once corporate names are removed, single keywords have low conversion rates, according to Oneupweb. Conversion rates for one-word keywords dropped from 32 percent to 7 percent when branded single keywords were eliminated from the data.

The lesson to be taken from this study is that you shouldn't optimize your site or bid on generic keyword terms like televisions, computers, or appliances. Instead, the data underscores the importance of integrating a range of keywords in a range of lengths into your site-optimization and pay-per-click bids. Yahoo! says that its Sponsored Search customers that bid on 20 or more search terms for their campaigns experience the most success in terms of traffic and conversion.

In addition to the keywords that you choose, a few other factors will influence your search marketing success. Most have to do with what happens after someone clicks on the search engine link and is redirected to your web site. Particularly with paid campaigns, you want to send search traffic to the deepest and most relevant page on your site. If someone searches for a specific product in a search engine, your link should lead that customer to a landing page that provides more details about the item and gives the customer the option to buy it. In other words, landing pages should match the search. Someone searching for a type of product should be redirected to that specific category page, while someone searching for a specific product should click through directly to that product. Customers will be frustrated if they're sent to nonrelevant landing pages on your web site and forced to repeat their search. They may immediately hit the back button without even bothering to browse your site.

Once you've lured searchers to your site, make sure they feel comfortable buying from you. The best way to do this is by having a well-designed and professional-looking site that is secure and easy to use. Search customers have likely never heard of your company before. So, you must use every weapon within your arsenal to prove that you sell quality merchandise and have a reputation for good customer service, and that you will respect their privacy, guard their financial information securely, respond promptly to questions or problems, and complete the transaction as promised. If shoppers have any doubts, they'll buy from another online merchant that engenders more confidence, and you will have wasted considerable time, money, and effort trying to acquire their business.

Pros and Cons

Search engines are some of your best tools for reaching potential customers. Most people begin their Internet sessions at search engines, and they count on the sites to lead them to the information and products they are looking for. If you're not doing things to make sure that your company shows up in search results, you're missing the opportunity to connect with potentially thousands of customers.

Thankfully, the search engines provide marketing opportunities for companies of all stripes and sizes, including those with millions to spend annually on marketing and those that can't yet afford to launch a paid search campaign. Both strategies—optimization and marketing—can be employed successfully to boost sales. But neither approach is easy.

Search-engine optimization is an evolving field and even the experts struggle to understand the algorithms that Yahoo!, Google, and others use to rank search results. Garnering better organic search result placement can be particularly confounding and frustrating for novices. Unfortunately, people who are inexperienced with the ins and outs of optimization may actually do things to sabotage their natural search rankings. Incorporating irrelevant keywords or repeating the same ones too often might result in your site being booted from rankings, as will the practice of "spamdexing," indexing identical mirror sites with the search engines. At some point, you may find it necessary to hire experts to help with search-engine optimization.

On the paid search side, there is the issue of cost. You can easily overbid on keywords and overspend on marketing in order to figure more prominently in the paid search rankings. Many merchants fail to understand the true cost of their search-engine marketing campaigns. As I've said many times in these pages, clicks don't matter nearly as much as sales do. With paid search marketing, evaluate not just your cost per click but your cost to acquire every new customer—that is, your cost per sale. How does that figure compare with your cost per sale on eBay and other marketplaces? If you're paying considerably more to acquire customers through search than through other channels, you may want to consider other methods of obtaining business.

You'll find that search-engine optimization and marketing are ongoing tasks. The search engines are constantly changing the algorithms that they use to rank web sites, and you'll need to constantly tweak your site to make sure that it remains relevant. On the paid search side, routinely evaluate the search terms you're buying to determine which ones are bringing you business and which ones are simply costing you money because clicks aren't converting to sales. This is definitely a facet of your business that must be managed.

Action Plan

Here's how to get your site placed prominently in the various Internet search engines:

- ✔ Index your web site with the three major search engines—Google, Yahoo!, and MSN Search—as well as the Open Directory Project and other popular online directories.
- ✔ Identify the keywords that are most likely to pay off for your business by reviewing your site content, analyzing your existing search traffic, and using the keyword selection tools provided by Yahoo!, Google, and other search engines.
- ✔ Boost the popularity of your web site by trading links with other Web publishers. This will improve your search engine rankings.
- ✔ Optimize your web site for natural search by incorporating keywords into category and product names, product titles and descriptions, and other content. Use keywords in meta tags, as well.
- ✔ Start a pay-per-click advertising campaign by bidding on keywords that are relevant for your e-commerce business. Bid enough money so that your ads show up at the top of the paid search results.
- ✔ Create compelling pay-per-click ads—again emphasizing keywords and common search terms—that will entice browsers to click through to your web site.

✔ Direct search engine traffic to targeted landing pages on your site, so customers can easily buy those products that they searched for from you.

✔ Make sure that your web site conveys the right image to search customers. On first impression, they should feel comfortable buying from you.

✔ Evaluate the effectiveness of your various search-engine optimization and keyword marketing campaigns. Tools from the paid search purveyors allow you to calculate your customer acquisition costs and return on investment for each keyword. You can use analytics services like ClickTracks and WebTrends to monitor the effectiveness of your paid and natural search campaigns.

✔ Experiment with keywords of various lengths and calculate which ones deliver the best return on investment. Drop high-cost and low-converting keywords in favor of those that bring you the most sales for the least amount of money.

Search Engine Success Story

Home Décor Products, Inc.

If there's one company that truly embraces a multichannel online marketing approach, it's Home Décor Products, Inc. (HDPI), of Edison, New Jersey.

Founded in 2000 by veterans from the kitchen and bath products industry, Home Décor Products now operates eight e-commerce web sites and often dabbles in other marketplaces. In addition, the company has muscled its way into the minds and wallets of consumers by harnessing the power of search-engine optimization, pay-per-click advertising, and comparison-shopping engines to drive sales and increase revenues. The company's growth trajectory has been so incredible that last year its chief executive officer and president, Michael Golden, was named Best Executive in the 2006 American

Business Awards, generally considered to be the Oscars of the business world. Under Golden's leadership, the company has expanded from one web site to eight, and revenues have grown exponentially as a result—to about $100 million annually. The story is even more impressive when you consider that in 2000, revenues were just $500,000 annually. And in 2002, the year Golden joined as a consultant, Home Décor was selling only 12 products. Now, that number is closer to 450,000.

Home Décor Products started in 2000 with just one web site, HomeClick.com, which remains its flagship. The online retail store sells more than 300 luxury-branded kitchen, bath, hardware, lighting, tableware, fireplace, outdoor, and home decor products, things that customers can't find at their local Lowe's or Home Depot. At HomeClick and its other sites, HDPI caters to the high-end home improvement market and what Golden has called "do-it-for-me homeowners," upscale buyers hiring contractors to make improvements to their homes.

The company's other sites all focus on a particular niche within the home-improvement category. Hechinger.com, an online revival of the old hardware chain, sells power tools, hand tools, outdoor equipment, building and remodeling tools, and welding and paint supplies. AbsoluteHome.com targets the mass market for home goods, selling everything from faucets and framed art to table lamps and tubs from leading manufacturers. Barbecues.com taps into the outdoor entertaining market with grills, furniture, and other outdoor products. KnobsandThings.com sells decorative home hardware, mostly high-end items that would typically be sold in showrooms, not home improvement chains. PoolClick.com sells a range of pool, spa, and hot tub supplies and other outdoor living accessories, including poolside furniture. ChefsCorner.com caters to gourmets and gourmands, competing with retailers like Williams-Sonoma and Sur La Table, by selling professional and high-quality cookware, tableware, appliances, and accessories. And finally, Cliquidate.com is a liquidation channel for HDPI to sell customer returns, refurbished products, and closeouts for its manufacturing partners.

These web sites are the company's main online sales channels, attracting 1.2 million visitors a month, about 2 percent of whom buy something within 90 days. Given this low conversion rate, HDPI relies on heavy traffic to sustain its business. The company frequently touts its brands through the search engines and comparison-shopping sites. "We want to make sure that when people are searching for what we sell that they find it," says Jeremy Dalnes, the company's marketing director.

"We market like a lot of Internet retailers do," he explains. "We use paid search to make sure that if people are searching for a category of product they come to our sites."

The company's products are also heavily indexed in two comparison-shopping engines, Shopping.com and Shopzilla. According to Dalnes, these sites tend to bring in a lot of business for HDPI, and the company sees a slightly better return on investment (ROI) for its spending in this channel versus its paid search campaigns. "That's mainly because you're able to qualify a user well in advance of them visiting your site," he observes. Another factor is that data feeds to the comparison-shopping engines are updated nightly so they reflect current pricing and inventory levels.

"The quality of your data is directly related to the ROI you will derive from participating," Dalnes shares. "It's imperative that you provide the cleanest, most relevant data possible, as frequently as possible."

To supplement these search marketing initiatives, HDPI uses affiliates to drive traffic and sales to its various sites. The affiliate program is operated by Commission Junction and includes more than 600 affiliates, many of whom operate home improvement web sites. To get the most converting clicks out of the program, HDPI provides product data feeds to its affiliates so they can promote specific items. In addition, the company will run sales and special offers specifically so affiliates can promote them. The company has affiliate programs for every web site but Cliquidate.com. It pays a commission of 6 percent to 7 percent on sales, depending on the particular portal, and on some sites, the average online order is $400 to $500. Top-producing affiliates for the flagship HomeClick.com earn more than $6,000 a month in commissions.

In addition to these strategies, HDPI uses other smart marketing techniques to capture sales. Each web site sells different products, but the sites draw from the same central database or catalog for inventory. That makes it easy for one site to refer customers to another. For example, a customer might search for a KitchenAid mixer at Absolute Home.com. Though the product isn't available on that particular site, it can be purchased on HomeClick.com. Instead of showing that a product isn't available, the search results show a sampling of mixers available at HomeClick.com and direct the customer to continue shopping on the other site. When a customer clicks on the hyperlink referral, a new Web browser pops up with a list of all available KitchenAid mixers at HomeClick.com. "We're not going to let that customer go," Dalnes says.

HDPI actively uses product recommendations and cross-selling techniques to generate incremental sales. Product detail pages and the shopping cart include links to related items that the customer might want to purchase. Suggestions are based on previous customer purchases, as well as recommendations by merchandising managers for each category. For example, someone buying a kitchen sink might see links for a faucet, garbage disposal, colanders, and other sink inserts and cleaning products.

The company actively markets to customers after transactions, as well, as a way of driving incremental sales. Customers who bought grills from Barbecues.com might receive an email offering a sale price on grill accessories or barbecue utensils. Customers are much more likely to respond to targeted offers that tie in to their previous purchases.

Finally, HDPI sells products on eBay and Overstock Auctions. Unlike many online businesses, HDPI came late to the auction space after building its own web sites and brand identity. Many online entrepreneurs take the opposite approach and sell in the established marketplaces first before building online stores. But HDPI takes a different view of these auction sites. They are not a primary sales channel, nor are they a focus of the company's brand-building efforts. Instead,

HDPI uses the auction sites as a liquidation arm for HomeClick.com, Hechinger.com, and the manufacturers whose products are sold on those sites. Customer returns, as well as manufacturer liquidations, are funneled to eBay and Overstock Auctions. HDPI wouldn't sell new products in these marketplaces, Dalnes says, because selling costs are higher than on the company's own sites.

As HDPI grows, the company continues to refine its marketing efforts to drive traffic to its web sites and improve conversion rates. "Essentially everything we do is to try to increase purchases on our sites," Dalnes says.

Video product demos and animated how-to instructions have recently been added to AbsoluteHome.com, using technology powered Easy2. By providing customers with more product data and the ability to see an item in use, HDPI is trying to replicate in-store shopping. The goal, Dalnes says, is to convince more people who are undecided or on the fence about a particular product to buy it from HDPI by providing a "more rich shopping experience."

At KnobsandThings.com, HDPI is trying to overcome customer indecision with a cabinet hardware sampling program. Customers pay up front for as many as three hardware samples to try with their cabinetry. But when they place their full order, they're issued a credit for items that they didn't choose, and are not required to send the unwanted items back. Only items priced at $20 or less are included in the sampling program, and customers must purchase at least $50 worth of cabinet hardware to receive credit for the unwanted samples. This program helps HDPI win the business of customers having trouble choosing from among several products. In the past, the company probably lost these sales to bricks-and-mortar retailers where it's easier to buy, try, and return items.

Its multichannel approach and unique marketing strategies tell only part of the HDPI success story. Detailed analytics have helped the company grow from a bit player in the home improvement industry into a $100 million behemoth in the span of just a few years. The company measures everything incessantly as a way of confirming that it is using resources in the best possible way and getting the best return on every investment.

HDPI uses a third-party analytics provider to measure many variables across numerous online channels and for a wide array of products. The company evaluates not just its advertising and comparison-shopping engine conversions and costs but the click performance of specific products to identify problems and opportunities. If a lot of people look at a particular product but don't buy it, HDPI executives want to know that's happening and figure out why so they can remedy the situation. When this happens with a product that HDPI lists in the comparison-shopping engines, employees may pull the item from the data feed until they figure out why sales are lagging. This prevents the company from spending money on comparison-shopping clicks that don't convert. The problem might be with pricing, the item description, the photograph, or some other variable. With more than 450,000 items in inventory, HDPI has to use performance measures like these to identify these types of selling anomalies.

More online retailers need to be keep track of metrics and leverage analytics to increase their conversion rates, Dalnes says.

"It's probably one of the most important things you can do as an Internet retailer," he said. "It will show you your opportunities. It will show your deficiencies and provide you with an action plan to grow the business. Without measures, you're making guesses based on what you think people are doing on your site."

Using the Comparison-Shopping Engines

As the Web has grown in ubiquity, more and more people are conducting routine business online. People use the Internet to communicate with their friends and coworkers. They go online to meet new friends and to find dates. They research vacation destinations and then book their trips online. They check their bank account balances, pay their bills, and shop over the Internet.

In fact, online shopping is the fifth most popular activity among Internet users. More than two-thirds of Internet users make purchases on the Web, and the popularity of online shopping has surged by about 40 percent since 2000, according to a comprehensive 10-year survey and study by the Pew Internet & American Life Project. These statistics support the explosive growth of the Internet as a platform for commerce and explain why so many new marketplaces and stores have opened up since the decade began.

This growth of online shoppers and marketplaces has spawned a different category of web site: comparison-shopping engines that help shoppers sort through the variety of merchandise and merchants on the Web to make smart buying decisions. These sites allow consumers to compare prices for the same item across a variety of different online retailers before deciding where to buy. Close to 50 million people every month visit comparison-shopping sites, according to Nielsen//NetRatings, and that's too large an audience to ignore. And usage is growing, at the rate of about 17 percent annually.

"Comparison-shopping engines have become more and more important sources of revenue," says Link Walls, a product manager at ChannelAdvisor, who helps his merchant clients navigate the comparison-shopping landscape. "It's definitely not a channel to be overlooked. As you're uploading your inventory to the Web, think about how you can present that on the comparison-shopping engines."

There are literally dozens of comparison-shopping sites operating on the Web, including general sites, niche ones, and even those that focus on local merchandise. Recently the industry has been undergoing some consolidation with the merger of popular sites like Shopzilla and BizRate and the purchase of other comparison engines by big companies. EBay now owns Shopping.com, and PriceGrabber is a division of Experían.

Shopzilla and BizRate.com, which run on the same technology and are owned by the E.W. Scripps Company, are the two most popular sites, together accounting for more than 30 percent of comparison-shopping engine traffic. EBay's Shopping.com gets about 18 percent of comparison-shopping traffic, followed by NexTag (10.2 percent), Google's Froogle (9 percent), and PriceGrabber (7 percent).

Read on to learn the ins and outs of having your products indexed in the Web's most popular comparison-shopping engines and the best practices for making the most out of these relationships.

Getting Started

Comparison-shopping sites work more like search engines than fee-based online marketplaces. Generally, you aren't charged to list your products with a shopping engine; you pay only when the site directs an interested customer your way. The amount you're charged for each lead varies by site, but it's usually in the range of 5 cents to $1 per click. However, if you want your products to figure more prominently in the search results, you can buy featured placement by agreeing to pay more for each customer lead. (Froogle is the only comparison-shopping engine that is completely free for merchants and that objectively ranks results based solely on search relevance.)

Now that you've decided to list your products in this particular channel, you'll need to determine which of the comparison-shopping engines provide you with the most traffic, the most buyers, and the best return on your investment. Because there are no listing fees— and virtually no risk to having your products listed on multiple sites—I recommend that you begin the process of having your items indexed on all of the heavily trafficked sites. After a test period of perhaps three months, you can evaluate your performance on each comparison-shopping engine and determine which ones you'll continue to list on.

Before your products will show up in the comparison-shopping listings, you'll need to register an account with each of the engines you have selected. Generally, you'll be asked to provide some basic data about yourself, your company, and the products you'll be selling. Some of the sites will require you to submit a credit card or make a relatively small deposit into a merchant account so they have a cash reserve from which to draft your referral fees.

Once you register as a merchant, most of the comparison-shopping sites provide you the option of completing a dossier where you can tell potential customers more about your company and your policies. It's a good idea to complete this step of the registration process because you'll want customers to have this information up front before they click through to your web site. Once someone clicks, you're obligated to pay the referral fee even if the customer ultimately decides not to buy from you.

Next, you'll need decide which products to include on the comparison-shopping engines. Some merchants choose to index their entire product catalog, particularly if they have inventory management software that makes it easy to upload bulk listings. If you don't have these capabilities, it's probably best to start small, perhaps by focusing on your best-selling items, until you determine whether you want to have a long-term presence on the shopping site. Once you determine which products you'd like to market on the shopping engines, you'll need to send a data feed to the sites. A data feed is simply a file that includes all the relevant information about the products you're marketing. In general, your data feeds should include photography, a title, description, keywords, pricing and shipping costs for each item, your company's home page, and a click-through address that will lead shopping engine customers directly to the product. By completing just these few simple steps, you'll have done all that's necessary to list your inventory with the comparison-shopping engines. But read on to learn how to get the most sales from your referrals and to make the most of your investment.

How It Works

Here's the best news about comparison-shopping engines: Even if you don't index your products, you might wind up on the sites anyway because most shopping engines send out Web spiders and crawlers to scan e-commerce sites for merchandise to include in their side-by-side comparisons. The things you've done to optimize your site for the regular search engines also will help ensure that your products are indexed for free. But don't make the mistake of thinking that's all you have to do to start receiving referrals from the comparison-shopping engines. Search-engine optimization might work for the small and free

Froogle, but not for large pay-per-click referral sites. If you want to receive converting leads from them, you'll have to pay.

In a nutshell, here's how comparison-shopping engines work: A consumer visits the site and types the name of the product he or she is looking for into the search box. The shopping engine searches its database for products that match that search and displays all matching items from a variety of merchants. These listings include a description of the item, a photograph (if the merchant provided it with the data feed), the seller's name and customer-service rating on the site, and the total price, including shipping and taxes, where applicable.

The comparison-shopping engines all use different methods for ranking search results, but the top three or four spots generally are reserved for merchants that have bid highest for placement. In this way, the comparison-shopping sites are very similar to regular search engines. They give merchants a chance to bid more than the going pay-per-click rate to have their products showcased. If the consumer in our hypothetical example clicks on a product in one of those top spots, the merchant pays more for the referral than will a competitor ranked lower in the search results. Statistics indicate that there's a reason merchants pay more for these coveted positions. Some sites report that half of all comparison shopper clicks go to the top three merchants listed in the category, regardless of other factors, including price.

You'll need to manage your comparison-shopping listings in much the same way you do your pay-per-click advertising campaigns. In fact, you may opt to bid on the very same keywords in both channels, focusing on those that deliver both click-through traffic and sales. As with search-engine marketing, it's important that your comparison-shopping clicks lead to targeted landing pages where consumers can buy the specific product they searched for. It's important that the information reflected on the comparison-shopping site is identical to that on your web site. That's why most comparison-shopping engines and merchants who successfully use them to drive sales recommend that you refresh your data feeds on a regular basis to reflect any changes in inventory, pricing, and shipping costs. "Merchants need to make sure that their data feed is as updated and as accurate as possible," says Tamim Mourad, chief product officer and cofounder of PriceGrabber, because neglecting this chore could result in failed sales.

Comparison shoppers use the sites to find bargains, and most of these customers make their buying decisions based on price. However, a few other variables can factor into their decisions. How a product is presented makes a difference; if your listing doesn't include a photograph or other necessary information, you're unlikely to win the sale, even if your price is the cheapest. In addition, shoppers often check out merchants' ratings before buying to see how they've treated previous customers. Finally, some comparison-shopping sites grant "trusted" status to merchants who achieve certain benchmarks. That designation can greatly affect how much traffic and how many sales that merchant receives from the comparison-shopping site.

Pros and Cons

The real advantage of the comparison-shopping engines is the exposure you'll get for your products. When you index your products in this channel, your inventory goes into a huge virtual mall where millions of motivated buyers shop every month. There are few places online where you can get that kind of exposure without incurring a lot of up-front costs.

"The biggest thing is the additional exposure," says PriceGrabber's Mourad. "You want to try to be in as many outlets as possible. This is an ideal venue to be able to be in front of a substantial audience and have a really good ROI for that marketing effort. You are paying to participate in a marketplace that has a large amount of interested buyers already coming to it."

Unfortunately, the comparison-shopping landscape isn't a perfect marketplace. It is very price-driven, and on all the sites except Froogle, money equals muscle. The more a company can afford to bid for specific keywords, the higher its products will rank in the search listings. What's more, it can be time consuming to maintain accurate product listings with the various comparison-shopping engines. Particularly problematic is the fact that each site requires different information in data feeds and files in slightly different formats. Sellers may find it difficult to manage listings with multiple sites unless they're using automation software to handle the job.

Contrary to the message preached by many of the comparison-shopping sites, price does matter. If your selling price isn't competitive, you will have difficulty selling products in this channel because buyers can always get the same item for less from someone else. To remain price-competitive, many merchants build in free or discounted shipping to their comparison-shopping engine listings. If you take this tack, make sure that you've factored this expense into your profit margin so you don't find yourself paying to sell items.

Comparison-shopping engines help smaller merchants achieve exposure that they might otherwise have difficulty attaining through their own web sites and marketing campaigns. This, of course, is a great advantage. However, because the shopping sites are so popular with consumers, they also attract retailers—brand-name companies like Home Depot, L.L. Bean, Amazon, Sears, and Circuit City—that may be able to offer better prices and also have the advantage of name recognition.

Finally, the comparison-shopping engines are helpful only if they drive real sales to your Web site. Some consumers use the engines to research purchases, clicking away on various listings in an effort to learn more about the product without realizing that each click costs a merchant money. As with any pay-per-click campaign, it is important to measure whether the clickers are converting to buyers, and if they're not, to assess why. Otherwise, you could spend a lot of money paying for traffic that doesn't lead to sales.

These caveats aren't meant to scare you away from the comparison-shopping engines. These sites are a great way to expand your company's reach into another channel. But, as always, it pays to be aware of all the risks of doing business in a particular marketplace.

Action Plan

Here's how to get your products listed in the various shopping engine sites:

✔ Familiarize yourself with the various comparison-shopping sites, particularly the top three—Shopping.com, Shopzilla, and NexTag—that attract the most traffic. Figure out which sites offer the best sales potential for your company

✔ Conduct a few searches to see if your products are already listed on these sites thanks to the efforts of Web crawlers. If your items are indexed, do they rank high enough in the search results to drive traffic to your Web store? If so, congratulations. You're enjoying all the benefits of the comparison-shopping engines without the expense.

✔ If you're wary of spending money in a new channel, first list your products in the completely free Froogle, a service of Google. That will give you an idea of how comparison-shopping referrals work.

✔ Establish accounts with the major comparison-shopping sites and start sending regular data feeds to them.

✔ Make sure that your data feeds are complete and updated with accurate pricing and inventory levels so customers don't get conflicting data when they click through to your web site.

✔ In the beginning, manage your expenses by agreeing only to the minimum pay-per-click rate for your particular keywords.

✔ As you gain more experience on the comparison-shopping engines, begin bidding more for the keywords that are most likely to generate sales.

✔ If you notice that you're getting a lot of traffic from the comparison-shopping engines, but not a lot of sales, examine your web site to determine what might be preventing people from buying. Are you directing buyers to your web site home page rather than to a targeted landing page? Is your checkout process overly time-consuming or difficult? Do you fail to offer customers the highest level of privacy and security protection?

✔ Track your return on investment with the various shopping engines. If some pay off better than others, you may want to focus your efforts there. Also, evaluate the seasonality of your shopping engine–driven traffic and sales. (Some merchants, for example, report that they achieve the best results in the fourth quarter of the year when people turn to the Web for holiday shopping.) If you notice similar seasonal patterns, you may want to time your shopping engine listings to take advantage of this.

✔ Collect contact information from your comparison-shopping engine customers so you can market directly to them in the future and avoid referral fees altogether.

Comparison Shopping Engine Success Story

ZipZoomFly

What a difference a decade can make.

Almost 10 years ago when two veterans of the computer hardware industry partnered to begin their own e-commerce business, their dreams and business plan were shaped by the Internet boom. The two partners named their company Googlegear—a variation on the mathematical term *googol*, which is the numeral 1 followed by 100 zeros. Their intention was to sell a vast and seemingly endless supply of assorted products, to be the sort of "everything *and* the kitchen sink" marketplace that Amazon.com has become.

But that goal was soon eclipsed by a more realistic one, and it's probably the reason this dot-com is still around at a time when so many others have failed. By 2003, the company had changed its name to Zip-ZoomFly and narrowed its focus to concentrate on performance computer components, which had always been the bulk of sales, anyway.

With all due respect, most of ZipZoomFly's customers are nerds—computer geeks and hard-core gamers who will spend whatever it takes to have the fastest, highest-performance system. It has always been that way, and the company has really embraced this crowd over the past few years, settling into a comfortable niche that brings in millions of dollars in revenues every year.

"In the beginning our customers were basically the computer geeks that liked to put together their own computers, tear them apart, and put them back together again," says Andy Wang, marketing manager for ZipZoomFly. "Now, they are also the gamers out there wanting the latest video cards and latest motherboards, everything to make their gaming experience more exciting."

With such a keen understanding of its customer base, ZipZoomFly, which operates an e-commerce web site at www.zipzoomfly.com, has implemented a very targeted multichannel marketing approach that pretty much ignores the mainstream marketplaces like eBay and Amazon. Instead, it emphasizes those channels that geeks visit when looking for computer components and electronics—namely, the search engines, comparison-shopping sites, and online news sites and forums that cater to techies. ZipZoomFly proves that it makes no sense to market your site outside of your niche or in marketplaces that aren't frequented by your core customer base.

"I think in the beginning we believed it was important to be everywhere," Wang says. "But now, that's not the case."

The comparison-shopping engines have become a big marketing thrust for ZipZoomFly, in large part because shoppers who visit them are so price-motivated. That works to the advantage of a company like ZipZoomFly, which uses low prices as a key competitive differentiator. Data feeds to these sites must be managed aggressively to reflect any new discounts or rebates that would rank ZipZoomFly as the low-price leader. Wang also monitors his company's click performance on the various comparison-shopping engines. Some shopping sites don't deliver much volume, he says, but their referrals are much more likely to result in sales.

Ideally, those high-converting sites are the places where he wants the company's inventory indexed. "You've got to compare the sites to see how fast your product is moving," he says. "If your product is really not moving, then there's no point in being there."

Without a presence on eBay, Amazon, or Overstock Auctions, ZipZoomFly's e-commerce web site is its only public face to customers. Much time, effort, and money have been spent to ensure that the site, which was built in-house, is as appealing as possible. But for computer geeks, appeal isn't defined by bells and whistles and fancy Flash programming. ZipZoomFly's customers crave simplicity, Wang says. They want to be able to find what they're shopping for quickly, and they want competitive prices. "Bells and whistles aren't what they really want to see," he notes. "They want to see what you have to offer. One of the things we decided from the very beginning was to create a web site that's more barebones. We made it as simple as possible for users to find the best products at the best prices." Such an approach may be contrary to the recommendations of many Web design gurus, but slick sites don't always sell.

ZipZoomFly's site opens with a very simple home page. There are seven navigational tabs at the top of the homepage, each of which points to specific categories of products, including computer systems, hardware, software, and networking gear. A navigation bar on the left side of the home page allows customers to drill down easily into specific product subcategories. The home page also gives customers the option of searching for a specific product or browsing by brand or special promotion.

A few carefully selected products do appear on the home page, and these are all accompanied by some special offer, such as a rebate, free shipping, or promotional pricing. The products featured on the home page change at least daily—and sometimes more often—depending on how quickly the items sell out. Many manufacturers request that their products be showcased on ZipZoomFly's home page, but the company won't break the rules for anyone. Over the years, the company has trained its customers to visit the home page often to find premier deals and special offers.

ZipZoomFly focuses on offering customers the shopping experience they desire, and a lot of things figure into that. Product selection, availability, and pricing are perhaps most important because repeat customers have come to view ZipZoomFly as a place to get the newest products at the best prices, Wang says. On some items, manufacturers dictate retail prices. But for others, ZipZoomFly sets the selling price, based on the wholesale price it is able to negotiate with suppliers and manufacturers. Because of the tight pricing structure and fierce competition of the computer components industry, ZipZoomFly has to offer a price advantage to convince customers to buy. Often, that's done through rebates or free shipping.

"In our purchasing department, we really follow prices and try to get the best deals possible from distribution. We literally watch these things by the minute," Wang insists. "You need to be able to monitor market conditions and pass that deal on to consumers."

Product information can be as important as pricing. Each item description includes a lengthy list of specifications, which details any unique features or benefits. In addition, ZipZoomFly often posts links to product reviews and manufacturer's press releases so customers can learn even more about the product they're considering.

From a navigation standpoint, the company is constantly striving to make its web site easier to use, and that has a direct impact on sales. Recent changes to the site's shopping cart now make it simpler and faster for customers to check out. For example, if the billing and shipping addresses are the same, customers aren't required to input the information twice. And there's a progress bar at the top of every checkout page so customers know how far they are from the finish line. "It might not be something that's revolutionary, but it is true that we're constantly improving the site itself so that the shopping experience, or even the browsing experience, is more friendly to the customer," Wang says.

Customer service, always a priority, has become even more so recently at ZipZoomFly in direct response to consumer feedback. Employees, including the CEO, read every comment that customers submit for hints on how to improve the business. In the past, customers lamented that they had trouble getting through on the company's customer service line and that ZipZoomFly was slow to respond to their questions via e-mail. That feedback prompted the company to change its policy for answering e-mails; now customers receive an automated acknowledgement that their question has been received and that an agent will follow up in a set time period with a specific answer. This gives shoppers a benchmark against which to measure response time. In addition, ZipZoomFly has upped the volume of calls answered daily at its customer service center by setting internal goals for its agents.

ZipZoomFly goes so far as to read the discussion boards and on-line forums where its customers hang out, both for product leads and to respond to any comments people make about their own buying experiences at ZipZoomFly. The computer geek community is particularly influential, Wang says, and people will make purchases based on recommendations they see on these message boards. "You would be amazed as to how effective or how compelling these types of feedback are to potential buyers of a product," he said.

Another way ZipZoomFly delivers on its promise of providing the shopping experience its customers want is through security features. Authentication and security are provided by thawte, Inc. and ZipZoomFly is verified by Visa as a safe shopping site. The company also displays its top ratings and certifications from BizRate, PriceGrabber, Shopping.com, and CNET Network to vouch for its legitimacy and trustworthiness.

On the marketing side, ZipZoomFly invests heavily in pay-per-click search campaigns and also goes in for more traditional Web advertising by displaying banner ads on sites that are visited frequently by its core customer base. ZipZoomFly ranks high in paid search results for the big search engines, but you won't find the company's banner ads on these sites. Instead, they appear on computer news sites, discussion forums, and newsgroups that attract computer tinkerers and professionals. The company's banner ads always reference a particular product or offer, as this greatly increases the likelihood of clicks and sales. The banner ads change frequently, sometimes as often as every week, to reflect new products or special offers the company is promoting.

In addition, ZipZoomFly sends out biweekly e-mail newsletters to its customer database. The e-tailer's newsletter usually focuses on a specific product—maybe something that has just hit the market—or a discount that is available only through the e-mailing list. The newsletter provides a direct link to that product page on ZipZoomFly's web site, so customers can buy in just a few clicks. Since implementing this straightforward click-and-buy format for its e-mail blasts, ZipZoom-Fly has seen about a 20 percent increase in sales of advertised offers, Wang says.

8

Advertising and Affiliate Programs

Up to now, this book has focused on how you can make millions in e-commerce—that is, selling merchandise to online shoppers. But the Web also offers another lucrative and legitimate moneymaking opportunity: advertising.

Visit virtually every web site—from search engines and travel sites to online newspapers and even your best friend's blog—and you're likely to see banner ads and other commercial endorsements on the page. In most instances, to have their products hawked on those sites advertisers are laying down cash, either by paying a flat fee every time the ad appears, forking over a few pennies every time someone clicks on the ad, or paying a commission for every click that results in a sale.

In the early days of the Internet, it was hard to make much money from online advertising. Even newspapers, whose very existence is driven by ads, struggled to develop a profitable revenue stream. Among other challenges, they had difficulty figuring out how to charge (and how much to charge) for banner ads, and had even more trouble convincing merchants to buy them. As the Web has become more ubiquitous, at least one of those obstacles has disappeared. Most companies now appreciate the role the Internet plays in attracting customers and allocate a portion of the overall advertising and marketing budget for online ads.

But that fact alone doesn't necessarily make it easier for Web entrepreneurs to develop an online advertising program. If you take the traditional route, you have to hire people to sell the ads, manage customer accounts, and create the ads. Given those obstacles, it's difficult for any shoestring web site to make money selling online advertising in the traditional way.

But when it comes to the Internet, the traditional way is often the *worst* way to do things. That's certainly true in the area of advertising. When you hear stories (including those in this book) about people who are profiting from online advertising, odds are they aren't doing it the traditional way. Instead, they're probably raking in cash as affiliates for online merchants or through programs like Google AdSense, which allows them to post relevant ads on their web site with relatively little up-front work required.

The great part is you can easily add advertisements to your site with little or no cost and generate recurring revenue for doing virtually nothing at all. This allows you to set up a site with free information for users that is funded entirely through ad revenue. It's also a potential way to bring in added revenue to your e-commerce site.

Elsewhere in this chapter, you'll find detailed descriptions on how the various affiliate programs and Google AdSense work. Just so you don't get confused before that point, here's a quick primer on both.

You've probably seen links to such companies as Amazon.com, eBay, Payless ShoeSource, and other merchants on a variety of web sites. Perhaps the links appeared as ads along the borders of the web page. Or maybe they were integrated into the site's content—for example, a book review that includes a link to the Amazon page where that particular novel is for sale. The Web publishers providing these links are most likely affiliates for the merchants, and they're receiving payment for every lead or sale they refer to that merchant.

AdSense works in much the same way. Businesses of all sizes, from small local companies to large global brands, pay to advertise through the search engine Google. Google, in turn, allows online publishers to post relevant ads for free on their web sites. The ads usually appear in a hyperlinked text rail and promote goods and services of interest to visitors of that site. Site owners who post the ads receive a few cents every time someone clicks on a link. (The advertiser ultimately pays the tab, but payments are distributed through Google.)

The search engine Yahoo! is testing a similar program called Yahoo! Publisher Network that would enable small Web publishers to post targeted Yahoo! ads on their sites. The project is still in the testing phase as this book goes to print and is by invitation only. You can visit http://publisher.yahoo.com for more information about this emerging advertising program.

Getting Started

Before you can make these affiliate programs work for you, you've got to whip your own web site into shape by working on the content, which will ultimately drive traffic and advertising revenues. If your web site doesn't have broad appeal (even within a niche category) and interesting content that is updated frequently or changes regularly, you're not likely to make much money through advertising.

In your own Web searches, you've no doubt stumbled upon web sites that are little more than link farms, filled with advertisements and links to other sites but containing scant interesting or relevant information. Many of these sites are operated by people looking for an easy way to cash in on online advertising and affiliate marketing programs. But they're unlikely to generate much revenue because they're not sites that people will remember or choose to visit again. Sites that subsist on advertising content alone are unlikely to generate enough traffic to support a successful affiliate marketing or advertising campaign.

Just as on television, in newspapers, and in magazines, advertising revenues are directly tied to quality of the content and audience for that content. For example, Fox can charge more for commercials aired during the ratings juggernaut *American Idol* than it can for ad spots on less popular shows. A big-city daily newspaper with paid circulation can charge more for a full-page advertisement than can a free, alternative weekly publication. Because of its high readership, ads in Oprah Winfrey's *O* magazine cost more than those in other less popular women's publications. By the same logic, a web site with heavy traffic—say a million visitors a month—will earn more from its affiliate relationships and advertising programs than one with a narrow audience of just a few hundred visitors a week.

"For affiliates, I really think content is the key," says Stephanie Schwab, vice president of Converseon, a digital marketing agency that specializes in affiliate marketing. She makes a point that is echoed by other affiliate marketing experts and entrepreneurs who have successfully leveraged online advertising in their businesses.

Before you start looking for companies to advertise on your site, commit to building a site that's rich with information and that appeals to the broadest audience in your niche. If you're really passionate about the New York Yankees, being a stay-at-home mom, or designer handbags, create a site focused on that topic. Then, build traffic virally, through word-of-month referrals, and by making use of search-engine optimization techniques like those you read about in Chapter 6.

"You want to keep working on that site because you really love the subject," says Shawn Collins, who stumbled into affiliate marketing in 1999 after creating an online diary about the birth of his first child. At first, friends and family members were the primary visitors to his site. But slowly, word spread and Collins' forthright musings about fatherhood began attracting a broader audience of other parents and soon-to-be moms and dads. Once he had captured an audience,

Collins began promoting relevant companies and baby products on his web site. These days, Collins runs several educational web sites for affiliates, owns an affiliate-marketing consulting business, and also manages the affiliate programs for Snapfish photo service and Payless ShoeSource.

"You want to have people that keep coming back to your site because they enjoy your voice and what you have to say," he explains. "Eventually the money is going to begin coming in as you build an audience." In other words, don't expect to start earning a fortune overnight. On average, you'll earn just pennies for every click, lead, or sale you send an advertiser's way. It's only once you've built up traffic on your web site and are delivering a high volume of leads that you'll start receiving big commission checks from affiliate partners and Google's AdSense division.

In conjunction with beefing up content on your site, it's wise to begin exploring other ways to market to your core audience. Savvy affiliates routinely send out e-mail newsletters that link back to their sites to drive return traffic to their web pages. This also increases the likelihood that visitors will see the advertisements and click on them, therefore generating revenue for you, the web site owner.

Web logs—or blogs are they're commonly called—serve the same purpose. They'll keep people coming back to your site over and over again—that is, if the information there is interesting enough and updated on a regular basis. "The best long-term solution is to have a content site that you're updating," Collins says.

Collins recommends using an automated tool, like AWeber Communications' autoresponder, available at www.aweber.com, to compile a database of visitors to your web site. On each of his web sites, visitors can provide an e-mail address and opt in to receive occasional e-mail updates and newsletters from Collins. The autoresponder allows him to send out automated messages to his readers at intervals he chooses. For example, when he had the baby diary site, Collins sent out personal reviews of different parenting books to the people on his mailing list. Readers received a new review every few days. Each message included links to Collins' own site and to affiliate partners like Amazon and Barnes & Noble where readers could purchase the books.

Now, in addition to his consulting business, Collins writes a well-read blog about affiliate marketing. Every time he posts a new entry on the blog, subscribers to his mailing list receive an e-mail teaser about the latest commentary. Again, the messages are sent out automatically with the autoresponder. AWeber Communications charges about $20 a month for its autoresponder product and offers discounts for quarterly, semiannual, and annual subscriptions.

These days, you can go just about anywhere on the Internet and build a site, even if you don't know anything about Web design. In fact, most Internet service providers offer easy-to-use templates that enable anyone to easily build a site. And thanks to the proliferation of social networking sites like MySpace, you can create your own home page with little effort or expertise. Such sites are fine if you intend them to be private places where you connect with friends and family. However, if your goal is to build a high-traffic web site that will appeal to a broad audience and eventually earn you money, you'll need to do better than using a cookie-cutter template.

Go to a site like whois.com or GoDaddy.com and register a domain name that will serve as your permanent address on the Internet. (The official web site for this book, for example, is www.TheOnline Millionaire.com.) Registration costs just a few dollars a year, and that price will buy you tremendous legitimacy and increased visibility on the search engines. It's also smart to invest some money in the design of your site. If you're not well-versed in Web design, hire someone who can create a clean and professional-looking site for you. Though you may blanch at the initial cost, the expense will pay off in the long run as your web page will be more attractive to visitors, as well as to potential advertisers and affiliate partners.

Once you've built a site that can support advertising, you can begin searching for affiliate partnerships. Most big companies, including Barnes & Noble, Amazon, Wal-Mart, and Match.com, have affiliate programs. In most cases, you can apply to be an affiliate directly through the merchant's web site. In addition, you might consider joining one of the affiliate networks that manage affiliate programs for multiple companies. The three biggest and best are Commission Junction (www .commissionjunction.com), LinkShare (www.linkshare.com), and Performics (www.performics.com). Also be sure to check out online affiliate directories like Refer-it (www.refer-it.com), AssociatePrograms.com, and Shawn Collins' AffiliateTip.com, which includes a monthly ranking of the top 10 affiliate programs. It won't cost you any money to sign up for a reputable affiliate program, so there's no harm in joining as many as possible until you find the ones that deliver the highest dividends for your web site.

Acceptance into an affiliate program isn't automatic. The best programs (those paying the highest commissions) carefully vet applicants. These companies must protect their own brands, and may reject applicants whose sites have limited or irrelevant content or are shoddily constructed. Generally, you should know within 24 hours whether you have been accepted or rejected for a company's affiliate program.

Signing up for the Google AdSense program is also easy. Visit www.google.com/adsense/, read the AdSense program policies, and complete a short application that asks for certain information about your web site. Once you're accepted into the program, you can begin integrating AdSense advertisements onto all your content-based web pages.

How It Works

Google AdSense and all affiliate advertising networks operate on the same premise: You get paid for displaying ads on your site for others. But how you're paid and how much can vary greatly from one advertiser to the next. Your commission is also contingent on what you do to optimize your web site for advertising.

First, I'll discuss how Google AdSense works because there are fewer variables than with affiliate programs. After you're accepted into the Google AdSense program, Google will provide you with a block of HTML coding to incorporate into your web pages. Once that coding is in place, targeted Google ads will automatically appear on your site in locations that you designate based on where you insert the coding. Each web page (remember that a web site is comprised of many pages) may include as many as three Google ad units, including text-based ads and banners.

Google uses sophisticated technology to scour a web site's content and, in turn, provide relevant ads—those that visitors to your site are most likely to click on. For example, at the web site of SeatGuru, a company you'll read more about later in this chapter, most of the Google ads are travel-related. SeatGuru rates airline seats based on legroom, comfort, and other factors. Wendy Shepherd, another successful AdSense and affiliate marketer who is profiled in this book, has several web sites targeted at busy mothers. The Google ads on her sites are usually for products that appeal to moms, children, and families in general. Of course, Google's technology isn't perfect, but it eliminates much of the legwork for Internet publishers seeking relevant ads for their sites because the process is all automated. AdSense participants also have the option of integrating a Google search box on their sites. This enables them to monetize results from Web searches, giving online entrepreneurs yet another way to cash in on the traffic they drive to other sites.

There are two ways to earn money with AdSense ads. Some advertisers choose to pay based on the number of times their ad is shown. This payment model is known as cost per thousand (CPM). But cost per click (CPC) is by far the most popular advertising payment model on the Web. In this scenario, an advertiser pays a fee when a Web surfer clicks on an ad. A nominal amount of this fee (usually no more than a few pennies) is paid to the Web publisher that referred the click. The higher an ad's click-through rate (a measure of the percentage of people who clicked on the ad after seeing it), the more money the Web publisher earns.

Now, let's talk about affiliate programs. Integrating affiliate ads onto your web site is pretty straightforward, as it is with Google Ad-Sense. Your affiliate partner will provide you with HTML coding that you can cut and paste directly into your own web site. On a web page, these strings of text will show up as banner, text, or image ads.

It's up to you to identify advertising partners that best match the content on your site. Because of that, you may have sign up for many different affiliate programs and test a variety of ads before identifying those that deliver the best results. In addition, you'll need to switch the ads frequently (either manually or through an automated process) to keep the content on your site interesting and fresh for visitors.

Like Google, some affiliate programs also pay per click, but most reward affiliates only if a referral leads to a sale or another action by the consumer. (The different payment models are referred to as pay per click, pay per sale, or pay per lead or bounty.) In general, affiliates earn less on click-based commissions than on sale- or bounty-based commissions, but clicks may be easier to generate than sales. According to the AffStat Affiliate Marketing Benchmarks report, which is based on a survey with 200 affiliate program managers, the majority of affiliate programs (77 percent) pay commissions only when the click results in a sale.

Pros and Cons

Affiliate programs and ad networks like AdSense are a low-cost way for web sites of all sizes to generate advertising revenue. It's clear from the proliferation of these programs that they are successful and lucrative for both merchants and Web publishers alike. Affiliates definitely are driving traffic to advertiser web sites. Depending on the merchant, affiliates generate anywhere from fewer than 5,000 to more than 500,000 click-throughs a month, with most activity concentrated in the 5,000 to 100,000 click-through range, according to the latest AffStat survey. On the flip side, affiliates are making money on the clicks and customers they send an advertiser's way. EBay boasts that its most successful affiliates earn commissions in excess of $25,000 a month, which calculates to $300,000 annually. And according to the AffStat results, 16 percent of pay-per-sale programs paid a commission of more than $20,000 a month to a single affiliate in 2006. (It's interesting to note that the percentages are even higher for pay-per-lead and bounty affiliate programs, with 49 percent and 43 percent, respectively, paying more than $20,000 a month to a single affiliate.)

Despite all these promising statistics, you're not guaranteed success just for signing up for an affiliate or advertising network. Conversion rates remain very low, usually in the range of 0.5 percent to 5 percent. This simply means that of all the people who see an ad or referring link on your web site, only about 0.5 percent to 5 percent of them will complete the action necessary to earn you a commission. (While some affiliate programs do report high conversion rates of 3 percent to 5 percent, on average rates are much lower.) The reality is this: To make money, your site must be heavily trafficked.

What to Watch Out For

Given these statistics, it's important to have realistic expectations of the revenues your advertising relationships are likely to generate. It may sound clichéd, but it's true. If an advertising or affiliate program seems to be too good to be true, it probably is. Established companies with strong brands and good reputations among consumers *may* be able to beat the industry averages for click-through rates and average commissions. But any affiliate or advertising that promises the moon and guarantees you'll get rich quick probably isn't legitimate. Therefore, you should avoid these programs and save your valuable Web real estate for programs that will pay, even in incremental amounts.

Beware if a company refuses to provide you with performance statistics, such as average conversion rates and expected earnings per click. Take its silence as a red flag, and look for a better partner.

"The only good reason why they wouldn't want to share that data is they have bad numbers," Shawn Collins insists. "Otherwise, they should be very forthcoming because they want you to promote them. I'm very happy to tell people what the potential is for the programs that I run."

Another important question to ask a potential advertising partner: What is the value of your average sale? Use that figure, along with the company's conversion rate and commission percentage, to calculate how much you're likely to earn from each sale you generate for the merchant. (Remember that most commissions are calculated based on the selling price, before shipping and taxes are added to the order.)

Here's an additional good rule of thumb: If you decide to partner with a company that you don't know much about, do only a modest amount of promotion for that company. That will give you a chance to see how well the ads perform on your site and ensure that the company pays you a prompt commission for the business you've sent its way. Keep it mind that commissions are usually calculated at the end of the month, and it may be another 30 days before you receive payment. If a company is slow or fails to pay, drop it in favor of a more ethical partner.

Initially, as I was outlining this book, I planned to include a list of the best affiliate and advertising programs. But as I interviewed experts in the industry, I realized that no such list exists, nor could one ever be compiled. The key to achieving success in this field is in finding advertisers that match your site content and that will appeal to your audience. For instance, the advertising partners that generate the most revenue for Wendy Shepherd and her family-oriented web sites wouldn't bring in a dime for Matthew Daimler at SeatGuru.

This may be the most important lesson you'll learn as you lease space on your site to advertisers. Not all of the ads will appeal to your visitors, and those that don't won't generate satisfactory revenues. You're in business for yourself now, and you ought to maintain detailed records of exactly where your income is coming from.

It is very important to keep track of which ads and partnerships are paying for you and which ones aren't. Fortunately, there are literally hundreds of other advertisers with whom you can partner. So, you'd be wise to drop those that aren't converting or paying high enough commissions. In addition, you should rank the prime ad locations on your web site. Does the banner at the top of the page deliver the highest click-through and conversion rates? Or are you making more money for ads that run along the right rail?

Eye-tracking studies have shown that people view web sites from left to right. They first generally look at the top left or center of the page, then read down the right rail before scanning the rest of the page. You can probably rely on general research when beginning an online advertising campaign. But once you have some experience and statistics of your own, analyze the data to identify the hot spots for ads on your web site. And remember, hot spots may vary by page. Your goal online is the same as if you were putting up a billboard along the highway. You'd want to choose a highly visible location with lots of traffic to guarantee that the maximum number of people see your advertising message and act upon it.

Many affiliate programs and advertising networks have tools that will help you analyze this data and rank your site's hot spots. You can also find applications on the Web, such as phpAdsNew, available at www.phpadsnew.com, that allow you to track your best performing ad spaces. Once you've identified these slots, you can fill them with ads that have the highest conversion rates and pay you the best commissions.

Action Plan

Follow these steps if you want to begin making money through online advertising and affiliate programs:

- ✔ Start by creating a content-based web site or blog that has the potential to attract a large audience.

✔ Alternatively, you can include ads for complementary products on your e-commerce site. (Just make sure these ads don't detract from sales of your own merchandise.)

✔ Tell your friends and family about the site and encourage them to spread the word about it.

✔ Market your web site through search engines and e-mail marketing, as well as other available means.

✔ Send out press releases about your site to specific reporters who would be inclined to write about it or broadcast stories about it.

✔ List your web site in relevant online directories. Also, make sure that other webmasters are linking to your site and referring people to the content you're providing.

✔ Sign up for accounts with Google AdSense, the major affiliate networks, and other companies offering affiliate programs.

✔ Begin integrating ads onto your web site, being careful to choose relevant advertisers that will appeal to your audience.

✔ Track the performance of the ads on your site to determine which partnerships are generating the highest revenues and which ad locations provide the biggest payoffs.

✔ Change your ad placement and experiment with other affiliate programs to determine the most lucrative assortment and arrangement for your web site.

✔ Continue to update and add to the content on your site so visitors have a reason to come back. Send newsletters and occasional e-mail messages to drive repeat traffic.

Affiliate Marketing Success Story

SeatGuru

As Matthew Daimler racked up frequent-flyer miles traveling between San Francisco and Prague, Czechoslovakia, an idea for a new web site was brewing.

Each time he found himself on a plane, Daimler made note of the amenities that his seat and the others around him offered. He was particularly concerned with things like a seat's pitch, legroom, and proximity to video screens, data ports, bathrooms, and the in-plane galley. Initially just for his own traveling comfort, Daimler quickly identified the best and worst seats on each plane. Realizing that other travelers would appreciate such data, Daimler created a web site, SeatGuru (www.seatguru.com), with rankings from bad to the very best of all the seats on the planes of the various airlines. "I thought it would be just a little web site that friends would know about," he recalls. "I never thought it would have a mass application. I continue to be amazed by its success and by how many people do enjoy and use it."

Indeed, SeatGuru is now an Internet success story. More than eight million travelers have accessed the site's comprehensive content for free. What's more, Daimler has succeeded with what many web site owners still struggle with: He has figured out a way to generate income through online advertising. SeatGuru, which is a private company, takes in well over $10,000 in advertising revenues each month and well over six figures annually. Daimler won't provide specific revenue or income figures, but he did share data about his web site traffic and pay-per-click advertising earnings. SeatGuru gets about 3.5 million page views every month. About 1 percent of those visitors click on an ad, earning Daimler 20 cents to 30 cents for each click. The site has been lucrative enough for Daimler and his wife, Susan, to quit their regular jobs and devote themselves full-time to this blossoming Internet venture.

It took three years, much trial and error, and some fortuitous publicity before either of the Daimlers found themselves in a position to give up a steady paycheck. Daimler kept his day job for two years longer than his wife did, joining SeatGuru as a full-time employee in 2006.

As Daimler built SeatGuru and got feedback from friends and other users, he started to realize just how unique the site was and how useful air travelers found it to be. As traffic picked up, Daimler began exploring ways to earn money through the site. His first attempt was by selling banner ads, with the hopes of generating enough money to pay some basic bills, like monthly Internet access and hosting fees. The ads were mildly successful, bringing in about $100 to $200 per month. But finding advertisers and maintaining those relationships required more work than Daimler anticipated. There was also the problem of attracting relevant ads. Many of the companies that bought advertising on SeatGuru in the early days did so only to improve their Google search engine rankings, which were based, in part, on how many other Internet sites linked to them. These advertisers weren't really interested in selling goods and services to SeatGuru visitors, Daimler says, so quite often the ads didn't complement the content.

Underwhelmed by traditional advertising, Daimler sought other ways to generate revenue on the SeatGuru web site. Acting on the advice of the owners of a popular travel deals web site, he signed up as an affiliate—or marketing partner—with all the major airlines and other companies, including Hotwire and eBags, that sold airline tickets, hotel rooms, and other travel services. Each company's affiliate program had different rules, but most paid a fee whenever Daimler sent them a lead or referred a customer who ultimately made a purchase on the web site. In Daimler's case, he expected to earn between $2 and $5 every time a SeatGuru visitor clicked through to an affiliate and purchased an airplane ticket, booked a hotel room, or reserved a rental car. "We'd get a handful of clicks," Daimler says. But his experience as an affiliate wasn't nearly as lucrative as the travel deals site's had been. "It never broke $35 a month, which is incredibly low, in my opinion. I thought it was a bust."

Daimler still isn't sure why his effort as an affiliate failed so miserably, given the success that other web site owners have had with this type of marketing. But he believes the answer might have something to do with the content SeatGuru provides—details about airline seats. Daimler estimates that most people who visit his site do so after they've already purchased an airline ticket and booked travel. By the time they log on to www.seatguru.com, these Web surfers are interested in choosing a seat on an airplane, not buying a ticket or reserving a hotel room.

Thankfully, Daimler didn't leave the game after the second strike. He continued to refine SeatGuru and look for new moneymaking opportunities. In 2003, he finally found one that worked for his business: Google's AdSense program. Essentially, Daimler leases space on the SeatGuru site to Google advertisers, and he earns money two different ways from the relationship. Some advertisers pay whenever a site visitor clicks on their ad; others pony up cash for every thousand times their ad is shown. Each payment is nominal, often just pennies, but when millions of people visit your site every year, the money quickly adds up.

When he signed up for AdSense, Daimler had doubts about how effective it would be. Most of the ads featured on the SeatGuru site pay only when visitors click on them and visit the advertiser's site. The cost-per-click model, new at the time, concerned Daimler because he didn't like the idea of showing ads without being paid for them. "I remember thinking, 'I sure hope that people click,'" he says. But because the ads are relevant to things that interest SeatGuru visitors—discount airfares, travel booking sites, and the like—people are indeed clicking through to find out more. "That's really one of the drastic differences in the marketplace: Having ads now makes sense to your visitors," he adds.

Daimler features one to three ads on each page of the web site, in order to maximize revenues. As a site owner, his work is minimal. He simply has to provide space for the text ads. "They give you the little piece of code to stick into your web page," Daimler notes. "The most work you have to do is determine where to put it on your web page. If you're capable of building a web page, you can do it."

As a member of the Google AdSense program, Daimler doesn't have to recruit advertisers. Google does that. He doesn't have to collect the money. Google does that. He doesn't have to sort through the ads to find ones relevant to his site. Google does that with its refined search engine technology.

"Google shows targeted ads reflecting the sorts of information and services SeatGuru visitors want," he says. "For a small business like mine, this is the best approach to advertising. You set it up easily, it automatically serves relevant ads, and it takes very little of my time."

Though Google does much of the legwork, Daimler is careful to monitor the performance of various ads in the respective placement locations. This enables him to make changes to maximize revenue.

Through his own experience at SeatGuru, Daimler has found that ads on the home page generate the most revenue, even though they immediately direct users from the SeatGuru site to the advertisers' sites. Daimler likens it to someone ringing your doorbell at home, then seeing something interesting in the neighbor's yard. Before you have a chance to open the door, they've gone over to the neighbor's house with the intention of coming to see you again later. "I don't really understand home page ads," he admits. "But they are still the top producers of ad revenue on our site."

Of the thousands of ads Google displays on the SeatGuru site, the click-through rate is only about 1 percent. That's not very high, but it compares quite favorably to traditional banner advertising, with a click-through rate of about 0.33 percent. It's clear from these numbers that to make money with online advertising, your web site must draw lots of traffic.

Because of his experience with the Google AdSense program, Daimler is able to more successfully market the SeatGuru site directly to advertisers. Though it doesn't happen very often, he will occasionally sell banner advertisements to companies outside of the Google network. Because of AdSense, Daimler has concrete data and proven results he can share with these other advertisers. He also uses the AdSense data to set advertising rates on the SeatGuru web site. Daimler charges his non-Google advertisers more per click or more per thousand impressions to post their ads on his site because he must expend greater effort to maintain these advertising relationships.

Daimler credits the site's popularity to its unique content, strong word-of-mouth following, and favorable publicity, as well as a lack of competition.

Soon after Daimler launched SeatGuru, another frequent traveler began building a similar site containing information about the seat configuration on international flights. Like the Daimlers, he was working on the site part-time and soon fell behind in his ratings of various airlines and their planes. As SeatGuru has gained more notoriety, others have tried to copy the site. In the company's five years in business, SeatGuru has compiled a database of more than 10,000 comments about airline seats, making it difficult for a fledgling copycat site to repeat. Some unscrupulous people have tried to steal SeatGuru's content outright. But Daimler had the foresight to copyright everything, and he can usually shut down those plagiarists with a cease-and-desist letter from his attorney.

With no viable competitors on the Web, SeatGuru is really the only comprehensive source for information about the airlines' best seats. Travel agents used to offer this kind of expertise to their customers, Daimler says, but that industry dramatically changed once online travel sites increasingly entered the mainstream at the start of the new millennium. "More and more people stopped using travel agents and were relying on themselves to book travel," Daimler observes.

Since it was a very young company, SeatGuru has also benefited from positive free publicity, in the form of articles in newspapers and magazines and mentions in radio and television travel shows. In October 2002, a reporter from the *Wall Street Journal* broke the story of SeatGuru, driving a tremendous amount of traffic to the site. "That was the first piece of press that we got, and I think it really put us on a lot of people's bookmark pages," Daimler says. "That really transitioned us from 300 to thousands of visitors a day."

Reporters remain interested in telling the SeatGuru story, and Daimler and his wife frequently consent to interviews. Every week, Daimler says, a major newspaper from somewhere in the country writes an article or blurb about SeatGuru. "There are always new people traveling or traveling more," Daimler says. "This is an ongoing interesting story." In fact, it's not unusual for the same newspaper to mention SeatGuru in three or four articles a year. Additional referrals come from the site's users, travel agents, the airlines, and corporate travel departments. Daimler wisely cultivates these referrals by sharing information about his site with these various entities. It's not unusual for him to even take calls from airline officials who want to learn more about how the SeatGuru rating system works and how they can configure their cabins to include more "green," or good, seats.

Daimler believes that SeatGuru's success is rooted in its content. It's why he's able to garner publicity. It's why millions of people visit the site every year. It's why he's able to earn revenue through the Google AdSense program. "We offer very compelling content," he insists.

The content, which is available nowhere else on the Web, keeps visitors coming back again and again. And it makes SeatGuru a popular venue for advertisers. As a result, Daimler is constantly striving to improve and increase the content on his web site by adding reviews of different airlines and new planes. These days, SeatGuru does much more than provide airplane seat diagrams. The site has become a clearinghouse of information for travelers, particularly those flying for business. Visitors can access comparison charts listing the seat pitch and width for every class of service in an airline's fleet. As a bonus for business travelers, these charts include information about whether the planes have video screens and power outlets for laptop computers. Additionally, the site provides information about the Transportation Security Administration rules on items that are forbidden and allowed in checked and carry-on baggage.

"I still think content is king." Daimler says. "You need to offer people something interesting on your site. It needs to be something that you're an authority on or that people can't get somewhere else."

Affiliate Marketing Success Story

Wendy Shepherd

Wendy Shepherd is living her dream, in more ways than you can imagine.

She works for herself, earning a six-figure income in a job that has allowed her to build a house for her family and homeschool her three children. Shepherd's adventure in entrepreneurship began in 1997, when her two oldest children were just toddlers. In what little spare time she could find between her child-care and housekeeping duties, Shepherd began cobbling together a web site of topics that interested her as a wife and mother. She built the site using free platforms on America Online and Geocities. Among the features she included was a list of helpful housekeeping tips. Almost immediately, Shepherd's web site visitors started responding to the tips, thanking her for the advice and submitting their own time-saving ideas. Traffic on Shepherd's hobby site started growing, as people passed along the URL to their friends.

Around this same time, Shepherd heard about an affiliate program—what was then a new concept to her—that paid 25 cents per click. Shepherd was a bit skeptical, but she did a little investigating and discovered that the affiliate program was legitimate. She also heard that other companies made similar payouts. "I found that even small sites can make money online," she says.

Shepherd made up her mind to turn her web site into a revenue stream for her family. She immediately registered a domain at www.tipztime.com, taught herself basic Web design and HTML programming, and set about building a site where other moms could come to get and share advice about how to manage a household. At the same time, she began joining affiliate programs, deliberately choosing companies that offered products and services that would appeal to busy moms, the core audience for her web site.

Money trickled in. It wasn't much at first, but enough to buy extra toys and clothes for the kids. Shepherd supplemented her affiliate income by selling yard sale supplies on her site and hiring herself out as a Web designer, again catering mostly to other moms.

The turning point came in 1999, when Shepherd joined Club-Mom, a social networking site where mothers share information and learn from one another. As a new member of the site, Shepherd received a welcome kit filled with chocolates, magnets, and other goodies for moms. Shepherd was so impressed by this gesture that she decided to begin promoting ClubMom as an affiliate. It turned out to be a particularly fruitful decision. Not only did Shepherd make $1 for each person who signed up for ClubMom through her site, but she also had the opportunity to meet the company's affiliate program manager, who became a sort of mentor to her.

Shepherd credits that man, Shawn Collins, with helping her achieve much of her success. When he ran the ClubMom program, Collins routinely sent newsletters to his affiliates aimed at helping them increase their referral rates. Shepherd read those newsletters voraciously and put Collins' suggestions to work on her site. One of his hints, in particular, really helped Shepherd grow her business. Collins provided a primer on integrating server-side includes (SSIs) into her web pages. SSIs are directives placed in HTML pages that allow you to easily add dynamically generated content to an existing HTML page. In this way, she was able to simplify the process of updating her web site and the hundreds of pages comprising it. Prior to using SSIs, whenever she wanted to make a change in the navigation of her web site, she had to open every page and make the same change over and over again. After following Collins' advice, Shepherd was able to streamline the process of updating her web site, giving herself more time to work on the content. Eventually, she was able to develop other sites with more targeted content, while cultivating additional affiliate relationships.

Shepherd now runs about a dozen different web sites, each targeted to a different niche audience—parents who homeschool their children, movie buffs, homemakers, shoppers seeking handcrafted items, entrepreneurs trying to achieve their dreams, and people seeking money management advice. Shepherd earns a six-figure income through affiliate links on those sites and by participating in the Google AdSense program.

It's important to note, however, that Shepherd does not include advertising or affiliate links on every one of her web sites. She first focuses on building the content to attract the largest audience possible. Once her traffic counts are strong, she then begins posting links for companies that sell products and services that appeal to her readers.

Find an audience first, then find advertisers, advises Shepherd, who has seen people fail by taking the opposite approach. A friend of hers once spent months sourcing retailers and building an online mall. However, he failed to capture an audience. When the online mall opened, there were no customers, and the venture failed.

Shepherd's two most popular (and profitable) sites are the long-running Tipz Time and Chart Jungle, which provides free printable charts for families. The charts cover a variety of topics—chore lists for kids, homeschool calendars, and auto maintenance schedules, just to name a few.

In addition to developing the content for these sites, Shepherd has channeled her efforts into scouting for the most relevant advertising and affiliate partnerships with the biggest payoffs for her business. And she's very savvy about incorporating these links into her own content. For example, at the Chart Jungle web site, Shepherd provides links to companies like My Reward Board, which sells software that parents can use to motivate their kids to do their chores and other tasks; ClubMom; Disney; 123InkJets, which sells printer cartridges; and Taylor Gifts, which sells a refrigerator-mountable magnetized organizer for keeping track of phone numbers, schedules, and the like.

To drive traffic to her most popular sites, Shepherd sends out weekly or biweekly newsletters, "depending on what's going on in my life." She maintains a database of more than 50,000 subscribers and provides incentives for people to sign up. Newsletter subscribers are eligible for free gifts and prizes, and they get the scoop first on new charts, tips, and helpful articles. These efforts, combined with a high ranking in the search engines, bring about 150,000 unique visitors a month to Shepherd's web site. (That number doesn't include her thousands of repeat visitors, who may come to a site like Chart Jungle every week to print out a fresh copy of a homework or chore chart.)

Shepherd pays as much attention to her online advertising as she does her content. She experiments with the placement of her affiliate links and ads, monitoring which locations and advertisements produce the most revenue. To keep her web pages dynamic and interesting for repeat visitors, she constantly updates the ads and seeks out new things to promote. For instance, Shepherd regularly trolls the ClubMom web site looking for information that might appeal to her readers. She might offer a teaser to an article of interest or a yummy-sounding recipe from her web site, in hopes that her readers will click on the link and sign up for ClubMom. (Every time someone does, she earns a commission.) "The advertising requires as much maintenance sometimes as getting content on your site," she says. "You always have to work the advertising. You must track it. It's like an online magazine. You should always have something new and interesting on there."

Shepherd is a member of about 100 different affiliate programs. Depending on the products and commissions the programs offer, she promotes them with varying degrees of zeal. But there's one other factor that plays a big role in how aggressively she pushes an affiliate's links. "I mostly work with those where the affiliate managers actually have contact with you," she says. Shepherd prefers to work with managers who treat her and other affiliates as advertising partners. The best programs publish newsletters with information on new products to promote and tips that will help affiliates improve their efficiency and increase their revenues, as Collins did for ClubMom.

The best managers are available to answer questions, Shepherd says, and they're willing to help affiliates improve their click-through performance and commissions. Remember, the more money an affiliate earns, the more business that affiliate is delivering to his or her advertising partner.

Another important thing Shepherd has learned in her nine years as an affiliate is that people don't immediately act on a referral. Site visitors will often click on an interesting advertising link, spend a few seconds at the new site, and then hit the back button on their Web browsers to return to her site. Many will return to the advertiser's site later on when they have more time or when they have a credit card handy. In fact, that happens all the time. Shepherd doesn't like to lose out on commissions from those delayed referrals.

That's where "cookies" become important. I'm not talking about chocolate chip cookies, but electronic cookies that enable a web site to recognize you as a repeat visitor. When you visit a web site, the server places a small data file, called a cookie, on your hard drive that will enable the server to recognize you when you visit the site again. Cookies usually expire after a certain amount of time—be it a few hours or a few months—though some may last indefinitely, depending on the site.

Many Web surfers don't like cookies because they're uncomfortable with the notion that someone is tracking their movements on the Internet. But cookies are very important to affiliates who want to be credited for delayed referrals. Generally, the longer a cookie lasts, the better it is for the affiliate, says Shepherd, who tries to work exclusively with companies that allow 30-, 45-, and 90-day cookies.

"I always try to avoid the ones with the one-day cookies," she says. And here's why: Say a mom logs onto Tipz Time to find out how to remove grass stains from her kids' clothes. A link for ClubMom catches her eye, and she clicks on it but doesn't take the time to sign up for the club because her laundry is waiting. Four nights later when the kids are in bed and she has some free time, the woman boots up her computer, goes directly to the ClubMom web site, and signs up as a member. Shepherd will still get paid for that referral because a cookie, which was stored on the woman's computer four days before, identifies that she came to ClubMom via Shepherd's Tipz Time site.

Shepherd still sometimes has a hard time fathoming how she became an Internet entrepreneur. Just nine years ago, she was raising two toddlers, living with her in-laws, and puttering on the computer in her spare time. She literally started out earning pennies at a time, maybe a few dollars a month. But even those small paychecks meant something to Shepherd because they were a testament to her ability to contribute to the household income. So, Shepherd persevered, while improving her skills as a Web designer, publisher, and affiliate. Before long, the pennies turned into dollars and the dollars into tens of thousands. Now, she is the primary breadwinner in her family. What's more, she's showing the world that there are many faces to entrepreneurism.

"I'm not just that little mom at home now," she says. "I actually did something that is raising eyebrows and helping to inspire people. Just because you're a mom at home doesn't mean you can't do something else."

Fifty Keys to Becoming an Online Millionaire

1. Invest in the proper equipment required to run your online business. At the very least, you'll need a speedy, high-functioning computer and a high-speed Internet connection. (Dial-up access just doesn't cut it anymore.)

2. If you want to grow into one of the Web's most successful merchants, be prepared to work hard and put in long hours. The Internet doesn't offer a guaranteed path to riches or success.

3. Pay attention to your feedback score on the various online marketplaces. If potential customers are unfamiliar with your company, they will use your feedback score to determine if yours is a reputable, honest, and ethical business. If you don't have a good rating from past customers, your sales are likely to suffer.

4. Familiarize yourself with the buying and selling practices on each of the online marketplaces. Most offer in-depth how-to tutorials and audio tours that walk you through the buying and selling process in step-by-step detail.

5. Make sure you have the right tools for selling on the Internet. Buy a digital camera with image-capture capabilities of at least 2 megapixels. Also look for one with macro capabilities, which will enable you to take close-up photos without losing focus or distorting the image. You may also want to buy special lighting and photography backgrounds to give your photos a professional

look. If you're selling flat items, like books, artwork, CDs, DVDs, and sports cards, a flatbed scanner may be a better imaging tool than a camera.

6. Make sure you have a PayPal account so you can accept electronic payments. Consider a Premier or Business account, which will allow you to receive credit card and debit card payments online for a small fee.

7. Register for a merchant account with your bank so you can process credit card payments.

8. Experiment with all the different methods of selling on eBay. Auction off some items, offer others at fixed prices, and sell some in your eBay store. This will help you manage your listing fees and squeeze out higher margins on certain items.

9. Tailor your pricing to the channel and product you're selling. If you're selling on an auction site and there's high demand for the product, consider setting the opening bid at 99 cents. If you're selling in a less heavily trafficked channel, set the price higher to ensure that you make a profit.

10. Use market research tools (available at online auction sites and from third-party companies like HammerTap) to determine the market for particular goods and to set reasonable prices.

11. Look for ways to minimize your selling costs by signing up for subscription selling plans and opening stores in marketplaces like eBay. Take advantage of special promotions offered by online marketplaces, like free listing days or discounted fees.

12. Create listing templates that include basic information about your business, including your contact information, payment terms, and shipping and handling charges. This will save you

time as you list inventory for sale, and it will also preempt many buyer questions.

13. If the marketplace offers them, take advantage of customized listing options that will bring attention to your products. If you really want your items to stand out, buy featured placement for them in the various marketplaces.

14. Offer your customers a variety of delivery options and always ship orders promptly, preferably within a day or two of receiving the order.

15. Invest in automation software that helps you manage your inventory and easily list products for sale in various online marketplaces. The best software will give you the ability to create listing templates, bulk list items for sale, manage inventory, process payments, answer customer e-mails, print packing slips and package labels, and integrate with your shipping company from a single platform. Choose software that can be used in all the channels in which you plan to sell.

16. Home in on top-grossing merchandise categories or focus on niche products that customers can't readily find at local stores.

17. Emphasize stellar customer service, which will help you stand out among competitors in crowded merchandise categories.

18. In marketplaces like Amazon.com and Half.com that give sellers a shipping allowance, make sure this amount is enough to cover your shipping and handling costs. If not, you'll need to raise your selling price to make up the difference.

19. Measure your performance against other sellers in the channel and in your merchandise category.

20. On Amazon.com, cross-link your products with other items in the Amazon catalog as a way of piggybacking on popular product searches.

21. Time your listings on sites like Amazon and the comparison-shopping engines to coincide with peak shopping times. These sites generally experience spikes in traffic and sales during the fourth quarter of the year when people turn to the Internet for holiday shopping.

22. Follow each marketplace's pricing rules and policies to ensure that your items aren't delisted. EBay, for example, won't allow merchants to list too many duplicate items. And Amazon.com does not allow third-party merchants to undercut prices on their own web sites.

23. Whenever possible, strive to offer your products at the lowest possible price. Include shipping fees in these calculations. Most Internet shoppers are motivated by price.

24. Negotiate volume discounts with shipping companies as a way of controlling costs.

25. Maintain a mailing list of current and previous customers and market to them via e-mail and online newsletters.

26. When building a web site, design it to fit your business now, while allowing for growth and scalability in the future.

27. List items that you're having trouble selling in free or low-cost marketplaces, like Yahoo! Auctions and Half.com.

28. Be consistent in your branding. Try to choose the same user ID in various marketplaces so customers can easily find you. When building a web site, choose a domain name that is just as recognizable and memorable.

29. Add content to your site that drives repeat traffic. Examples are blogs, glossaries, buying guides, independent product reviews, and discussion forums.

30. On auction sites where fraud is a concern, block bidders with low or negative feedback ratings. Report nonpaying bidders so you can recover auction closing fees, and leave negative feedback to warn others about deadbeat buyers and sellers.

31. Publicize your feedback ratings and reputations across various marketplaces. If you're a highly rated veteran eBay seller, reference that on your web site, in your seller profiles, and in other channels.

32. Sign up for third-party verification and rating services such as VeriSign, buySAFE, BizRate, thawte, and others. Displaying these credentials will engender greater consumer confidence and increase the likelihood that people will buy from you.

33. Use keyword selection tools from Google and Yahoo! to determine if there's an online market for what you're selling and to get ideas for keywords to use in your search-engine optimization and pay-per-click advertising campaigns.

34. When designing an e-commerce store, create an outline to plan the site's navigation and other necessary elements.

35. Consult Web ratings from such companies as Hitwise and Nielsen//NetRatings and visit traffic-tracking sites like Alexa to evaluate the viability of an online channel. In general, traffic equals customers.

36. Get a business credit card and/or bank account so you can easily keep track of business expenses for tax purposes. In some cases, a business line of credit might be a good idea.

37. At each online marketplace, take time to customize your seller information and selling preferences.

38. Join groups like the Professional eBay Sellers Alliance (PeSA) and the Trusted Overstock Auction Sellers Affiliate (TOASA). You may earn special perks because of membership in these groups, and you'll also benefit from networking with other professional online sellers.

39. Regularly update your data feeds to the comparison-shopping engines so that they reflect your current pricing and inventory levels.

40. Aim to show up in the top three listings with the comparison-shopping engines because statistics show these spots generate the most clicks.

41. Make sure your comparison-shopping and search-engine clicks lead to targeted landing pages where customers can buy the specific item they searched for.

42. List your full product catalog on the Froogle shopping engine. To save money, list only best-selling items on the paid comparison-shopping engines.

43. With your natural and paid search-engine campaigns, your goal should be for your web site to appear on the first screen of listings because consumers are more likely to click on those links.

44. Index your web site with the three major search engines and list it in the Open Directory Project.

45. Incorporate as many relevant keywords as possible into the text of your web site, as well as in the hidden Web coding that is visible to the search engines.

46. Set a daily budget for your pay-per-click advertising campaigns to keep costs under control.

47. Remember that more specific and descriptive keywords result in higher conversion rates and more sales.

48. Avoid common pitfalls of search-engine optimization. Incorporating irrelevant keywords or repeating the same ones too often might result in your web site being booted from search engine rankings, as will the practice of "spamdexing," indexing identical mirror sites with the search engines.

49. Join the three major affiliate networks—Commission Junction, LinkShare, and Performics—to expand your online presence.

50. To successfully generate revenue as an affiliate, make sure to update the content on your web site frequently so it remains interesting and relevant enough to attract visitors.

Networking Groups for Online Sellers

Professional eBay Sellers Alliance (PeSA)
www.gopesa.org

Trusted Overstock Auction Sellers Affiliate (TOASA)
www.toasa.org

Online Auction Sites

Audiogon
www.audiogon.com

Bid4Assets
www.bid4assets.com

Bidville
www.bidville.com

CigarBid
www.cigarbid.com

eBay
www.ebay.com

eBid
www.ebid.com

ePier
www.epier.com

FaithBid
www.faithbid.com

iGavel
www.igavel.com

iOffer
www.ioffer.com

OnlineAuction
www.onlineauction.com

OnSale
www.onsale.com

Overstock Auctions
www.auctions.overstock.com

PBA Galleries
www.pbagalleries.com

PenBid
www.PenBid.com

Property Room
www.propertyroom.com

Sell.com
www.sell.com

uBid
www.ubid.com

Wagglepop
www.wagglepop.com

WhaBam
www.whabam.com

Yahoo! Auctions
www.auctions.yahoo.com

Other Resources

Alexa
www.alexa.com

AWeber's autoresponder e-mailing program
www.aweber.com

Google Toolbar
http://toolbar.google.com

Open Directory Project
www.dmoz.org

Keyword Selection Tools

Wordtracker
www.wordtracker.com

Yahoo! Keyword Selector Tool
http://searchmarketing.yahoo.com/rc/srch

Advertising and Affiliate Resources

Associate Programs
www.associateprograms.com

Commission Junction
www.commissionjunction.com

Google AdSense
www.google.com/adsense

LinkShare
www.linkshare.com

Performics
www.performics.com

phpAdsNew
www.phpadsnew.com

Refer-it
www.refer-it.com

Shawn Collins' Affiliate Tip Newsletter
www.affiliatetip.com

Search Engine Marketing Resources

ClickTracks
www.clicktracks.com

WebTrends
www.webtrends.com

Channel Management and Automation Software

Andale
www.andale.com

Auction Wizard 2000
www.auctionwizard2000.com

ChannelAdvisor
www.channeladvisor.com

ChannelMax
www.channelmax.net

eBay Developers Program
http://developer.ebay.com

Infopia
www.infopia.com

Kyozou
www.kyozou.com

Marketworks
www.marketworks.com

Meridian
www.noblespirit.com

Monsoon
www.monsoonworks.com

SellerEngine
www.sellerengine.com

Seller's Assistant Pro
www.ebay.com

SpareDollar
www.sparedollar.com

Truition
www.truition.net

Turbo Lister
www.ebay.com

Vendio
www.vendio.com

Zoovy
www.zoovy.com

Online Payment and Payment-Processing Companies

PayPal
www.paypal.com

Required Reading

Auctionbytes newsletter for auction sellers
www.auctionbytes.com

The eBay Millionaire (John Wiley & Sons, 2005)
www.TheOnlineMillionaire.com

The eBay Billionaires' Club (John Wiley & Sons, 2007)
www.TheOnlineMillionaire.com

Acknowledgments

Writing a book is never an easy task, nor is it easy to live with someone while they're writing a book. My husband, Bruce, as always, stood by me and helped in every way imaginable as I was working on this manuscript.

Typically, I thank Bruce last for his help and support, but this time he gets top billing because he so skillfully juggled our household and my demands as I simultaneously wrote this book and journeyed through three trimesters of pregnancy. Even when he would come home exhausted from his own job, Bruce never complained when I asked him to make dinner, move furniture, or make a midnight run to the convenience store to satisfy some craving. He indulged me when I postponed plans so I could get more work done and when I kicked him out of our home office so I could write. Truly, without his help, these pages would be blank.

I also owe special thanks to Kirk Kazanjian of Literary Productions, who gave me flexible deadlines and never doubted my ability to finish this manuscript. At least one of us had that confidence!

On any project, certain people go above and beyond the call of duty. Such was the case with several of my sources for *The Online Millionaire*, who not only shared their success stories with me, but also helped me to identify other great online entrepreneurs to include in the book. I feel particularly grateful to Charlene and Frank Lee of Fleegolf, Michael Jansma of GEMaffair, Kevin Harmon of Inflatable Madness, Shawn Collins of Shawn Collins Consulting, and the staff at ChannelAdvisor. You provided a great road map for me to follow. Thank you all very much.

A. J.